MEXICAN AM
BASEBALL IN
CENTRAL COAST

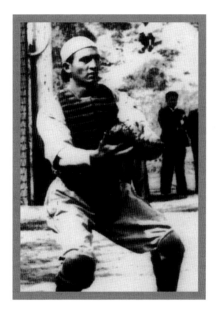

Richard A. Santillán with Christopher Docter,
Anna Bermúdez, Eddie Navarro, and Alan O'Connor
Foreword by Jorge Iber

ARCADIA
PUBLISHING

Copyright © 2013 by Richard A. Santillán
ISBN 978-1-4671-3087-5

Published by Arcadia Publishing
Charleston, South Carolina

Printed in the United States of America

Library of Congress Control Number: 2013940521

For all general information, please contact Arcadia Publishing:
Telephone 843-853-2070
Fax 843-853-0044
E-mail sales@arcadiapublishing.com
For customer service and orders:
Toll-Free 1-888-313-2665

Visit us on the Internet at www.arcadiapublishing.com

A Teresa, eres mi pedazo de cielo (Richard)
For my dad, Richard Docter, and grandparents Robert and Diane Docter (Christopher)
To my husband, Mario, and to my grandson Justin Joseph, who plays ball as his tíos did: for the love of the game (Anna)
To my coaches Johnny and Milt Guggia, Lou Borges, Don Mosier, Bill Yánez, and all youth coaches who teach the game by example (Eddie)
Thanks to Sacramento's Mexican American baseball community for educating and inspiring me (Alan)

4/14

796.35709
Santilla¦ün, Richard A.
Mexican American baseball in the
Central Coast /
-¬2013.

Discarded by
Santa Maria Library

MEXICA
BASEBALL IN THE
CENTRAL COAST

"Béisbol" (2013)

The ball was constructed out of rags and sticks
It was constructed the same way frijoles and arroz were made
With naked hands all the heat in the world all the trails norte
Caravans & plows cotton and grapes fire and snow
No one complained some stayed behind some noticed
Something ahead they could not describe

They made tortillas & burritos on the baseball field
On the side while the players prepared
Load up the ramflas charter buses llégale on Friday night or Sábado
Wacha la familia los compás y dale al borlo con ref
Píchale
Pégale duro Rudy!
Ponchatalo Lupita!
Aye vienen los jugadores!
If you don't hit a homer my abuelita te va a dar un palazo con el palote!

If there is pain or scars and the hurt from yesterday
We will swing it out of the parkeh
The fields are clean & las familias are gathering
& the tortillas are smelling good & wait till you catch the frijoles
We will pour out our voices & pick up the ball
Where we left it last time & begin again

Juan Felipe Herrera has published nearly 30 books of poems and stories. He is the 2012–2014 poet laureate of California.

FRONT COVER: Ernie Cervantes, shown here in 1940, was known as "Mr. Baseball" within the Sacramento Mexican American community. He was good enough to be offered a professional contract with the St. Louis Browns. His four sons and daughter followed in his baseball footsteps. (Courtesy of Ernie Cervantes Jr.)

COVER BACKGROUND: A visiting Cuban team played in Baldwin Park, California, around 1932. The folklórico dance group, known as the Princesses, was comprised of local young women, including Natividad Rodríguez. (Courtesy of the Linda Quiroz Archives.)

BACK COVER: Mason Covarrubias (first row, third from left) played baseball for the Golden State Dairy team in Oxnard in 1930. Covarrubias's father owned a saddle and harness shop near downtown, and the family lived in a large house with a big backyard. His son Chuck remembers hundreds of people showing up at the house for the yearly autumn barbecues. (Courtesy of Museum of Ventura County.)

CONTENTS

FOREWORD

Recounting and documenting resistance to oppression has, from the start of Mexican American studies, been key goals. It is logical to research such efforts in the struggle for educational equality, labor rights, political participation, and immigration reform, but can sports contribute to this narrative? Not surprisingly, mainstream scholars of athletics and sports management have argued that Mexican Americans would not make good athletes. Fortunately, the Mexican American community can now confront this fallacy with irrefutable evidence, showing yet another avenue of resistance and pride.

In 2001, Dr. Richard Santillán at California State University at Pomona published an article on Mexican American baseball in Midwestern barrios. He noted that baseball had a cultural, political, and labor significance. Fascinated, I contacted him and, soon thereafter, commenced my own research on high school football and its impact on Mexican American life in Texas. That kernel has now grown to several works, including wrestling and baseball, that help reveal an overlooked aspect of our rich history prior to the 1960s.

In addition to having historical significance, sports are crucial to current Mexican Americans. In countless communities throughout the nation, Mexican Americans are making their mark on courts, mats, tracks, and fields. These offspring of prior generations proudly represent towns that had previously thought of them only as workers in low-paying industries. While much is being done on the historical linkage between Mexican Americans and sports, more remains to be discovered; for example, the role of *mujeres* (women) and biographies of significant *atletas* (this author is currently working on the story of Mike Torrez).

The Latino Baseball History Project is promoting the importance of baseball and softball, and the more we learn, the more sense we can make of the current athletic opportunities for our sons and daughters. This new book continues this worthy undertaking and shows that, no matter where they settled, Mexican Americans enjoyed and utilized baseball to improve daily life. These works are just the start, for there are myriad locales (such as Texas!) to examine sport's immense value to Mexican American life.

—Dr. Jorge Iber
Associate Dean of Arts and Sciences and Professor of History
Texas Tech University, Lubbock, Texas

ACKNOWLEDGMENTS

The foundation of this project to publicize the rich history of Mexican American baseball and softball in the Central Coast is due to the remarkable work of the Latino Baseball History Project at California State University, San Bernardino (CSUSB). Others who supported this effort include the following individuals and staff at CSUSB's John M. Pfau Library: Dean Cesar Caballero and Sue Caballero, Jill Vassilakos-Long (head of archives and special collections), Iwona Contreras, Ericka Saucedo, Amina Romero, Carrie Lowe, Manny Veron, Brandy Montoya, Hayley Parke, John Baumann, and Stacy Magedanz.

The authors are grateful to the players and their families who provided cherished photographs and remarkable oral histories. These dedicated individuals and groups include the following: Margaret Villa Cryan, Ronnie Villa, Linda Herrera, Gene Pico, James Henninger Aguirre, Camilia López, the Orozco family, Ronald W. Venegas, Darcy Quinlan Meyer, Tim Ramos, John Y. Dickinson III, Lionel García, Sonny Benavidez, Rod Martínez, Isabel Ramírez, Louis Vásquez, Mike Cervantes, Dick Alejo, Cuno Barragán, Phil Barros, Pete Campos, Eddie Cervantes, Eric Cervantes, Ernie Cervantes Jr., Ricardo Cortes Costello, Tom Crisp, Joe Duarte, Jim Fellos, Ed García, Hank López, Tom Ramírez, Julius Resendez, Frank Ríos, Gil Urbano, Charles Johnson, John Keefe, Chuck Covarrubias, Frank P. Barajas, José Alamillo, Mario Bermúdez, Frank Moraga, Antonio Magaña, Michele Serros, Ed and Lou Ybarra, Alex Muñoz, Becky and Ernie Morales, Sandra Davis Gunderson, Irma López, Richard Félix García, Sam and Annie Salas, Dan Díaz, Joe García Jr., Ramona Valenzuela Cervantes, Mike Velarde, Isabel Vaiz Mejia, Mike Ramírez, Rita Delgado, Vickie Carrillo Norton, Joe Govea, Richard Arroyo, Alice Cruz Bacon, Terry Bacon, David García, Everto Ruiz, Richard Docter, Ernie Corral, Al Ramos, Joe Talaugon, Shirley Contreras, Bill Rule, Hilda Salto, Bobby Martínez, the Ray Orosco family, John Villa, Bill Miller, Al Truscio, John Rodríguez, Rennie Pili, John Lizalde, Betty Silva Smith, Tony Viegas, Hank Curaza, Maria Navarro, Mickey Pardo, James Bartlett, Bill Libbon, Pete Brumana, Paul Béndele, Art Amarillas, Rudy Galván, John Jiménez, Blas Torres, Art Manríquez, Tets Furukawa, Albert Rodríguez, Bill Righetti, Henry Flores, Ed Arellano, Carmen Nevarez, Steve Oquendo, Steve Martínez, Mario Montecino, Felix Olguin, the Botello family, Rosemary Andrade and Steve Binder, Houston Public Library, Montebello Historical Society, Texas A&M University–Corpus Christi, Señoras of Yesteryear, Sacramento Mexican American Hall of Fame, Museum of Ventura County, California State University Channel Islands, San Fernando Museum of Art and History, San Fernando Historical Society, Santa Maria Historical Museum, Santa Maria City Library, Guadalupe Cultural Arts and Education Center, Guadalupe Sports Hall of Fame, and the Lompoc Historical Society. Any uncredited photographs appear courtesy of the Latino Baseball History Project.

A special thanks to Mark Ocegueda, who wrote chapter six, on the Inland Empire. We recognize the incredible work of our editor, Elisa Grajeda-Urmston, and offer special appreciation to our technical consultant Abel Becerra. Last but not least, we salute Arcadia Publishing and our outstanding editor, Jared Nelson.

INTRODUCTION

Mexican Americans have played baseball in the United States for over 140 years. The sport was an important part of the overall Mexican experience in the country. This book examines the love of the game by Mexican Americans in the greater Central Coast of California. Mexicans lived in California prior to statehood in 1850. Both Spanish and Mexican cultural influences are profoundly evident throughout the greater Central Coast, including geographical designations, architecture, city and street names, missions, foods, language, traditional holidays, and customs celebrated by the people.

The Mexican people from the greater Central Coast can be found in various communities, including Oxnard, Fillmore, Ojai, Santa Paula, Camarillo, Piru, Ventura, Carpinteria, Santa Barbara, Goleta, Santa Maria, Guadalupe, Lompoc, San Inez, and Pismo Beach. Like so many Mexican communities at the turn of the 20th century, these neighborhoods established an elaborate infrastructure that included religious groups, business associations, mutual aid societies, civil and political rights organizations, fine arts, Spanish-language newspapers, legal aid, labor unions, and sports clubs.

Mexican Americans enjoyed baseball, softball, boxing, football, soccer, and basketball. Yet, baseball, and later softball, stood head and shoulders above the other sports. Baseball was played in Mexico by the late 1800s, and many Mexicans continued their love for the game when they settled throughout the United States. Players and their families helped create the economic infrastructure and prosperity that is evident in the Central Coast today, whether it was laboring in the fields, factories, packinghouses, or on the railroads.

For women, softball served as a social counterbalance to the strict cultural roles defined in their time. Many former players, men and women, devoted their lives to the unrelenting struggle for social, political, cultural, and gender equality, while others dedicated themselves to youth sports. Sunday was a special day for Mexican American communities, with religious services in the morning and baseball in the afternoon. This book relives those glorious days when Mexican foods were enjoyed and the Spanish language was heard at ballparks throughout the Central Coast.

SAN FERNANDO VALLEY

In 1933, noted UCLA geography professor Clifford M. Zierer wrote that Mexican Americans in San Fernando played "on numerous vacant lots . . . [with] improvised grandstands for baseball." Zierer's observation gives a snapshot into the vibrant Mexican American baseball and softball scene in the San Fernando Valley throughout the first half of the 20th century, an era tinged with discrimination. In San Fernando, Mexican Americans were prohibited from buying a home outside the southwest section of the city, beyond the Southern Pacific railroad tracks, and had to sit in the balconies of theaters. In Burbank, they could not live above Glenoaks Boulevard and were not allowed in the Pickwick swimming pool and certain movie theaters. In the face of these restrictions, Mexican Americans improvised and asserted themselves in the community, owning cafés, pool halls, grocery stores, nurseries, contracting companies, waste-management companies, selling produce and materials from their gardens, and playing sports. Mexican American baseball and softball teams literally carved out their own public space—plowing, raking, watering, and fencing vacant fields, transforming them into baseball diamonds.

Men and women in the Valley participated in a variety of semipro, municipal, barrio, and Catholic baseball and softball leagues. Many players participated on military teams while serving in World War II and Korea. By the 1950s and 1960s, Mexican Americans made significant inroads into Little League, Pony League, and high school teams, with a few breaking into professional baseball.

Teams in the San Fernando Valley did not live in a bubble but often travelled throughout California and Mexico. Many of the area's Mexican American families were connected to Central and Northern California as seasonal agricultural workers. In "going up north," families traveled to areas such as Fresno, Gilroy, and San Jose to harvest apricots, walnuts, peaches, grapes, cherries, and prunes. Likewise, players and families constantly rumbled north in dusty trucks for weekend games along the Central Coast in Santa Barbara and Santa Maria, reaching as far as Fresno. These trips further strengthened interregional community bonds through after-game celebrations, barbeques, and music honoring visiting teams. Extensive trips to the north helped instill solidarity among Mexican American ballplayers throughout California.

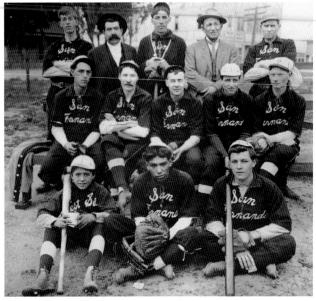

Seen here around 1909, the San Fernando team included batboy Edward Lyon (first row, left), Albert García (first row, center), Fred Candelot (second row, far left), and Raúl Candelot (third row, third from left). Frank Pico (third row, second from left) served as manager. A descendant of the prominent Pico family, Frank's grandfather Jose De Jesús Pico was the grantee of Rancho Piedra Blanca in San Luis Obispo County and cousin of Pio Pico. (Courtesy of the San Fernando Valley Historical Society.)

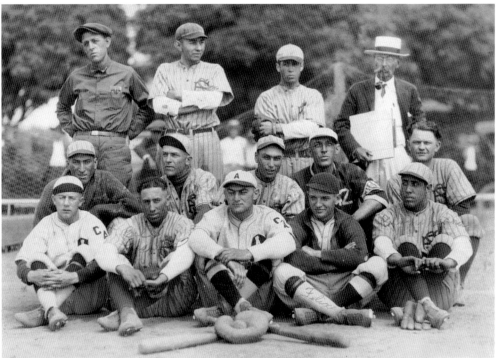

The 1922 San Fernando Merchants pose for a team photograph. Shown here are, from left to right, (first row) unidentified, Bill Pesqueira, two unidentified players, and Refugio Zamora; (second row) Frank Cruz, Arthur Lyon, Paul Cruz, Raúl Candelot, and unidentified; (third row) Fred Candelot, George Bravo, Ignacio Pesqueira, and unidentified. Bravo and Lyon served in France during World War I. (Courtesy of Vickie Carrillo Norton and the San Fernando Valley Historical Society.)

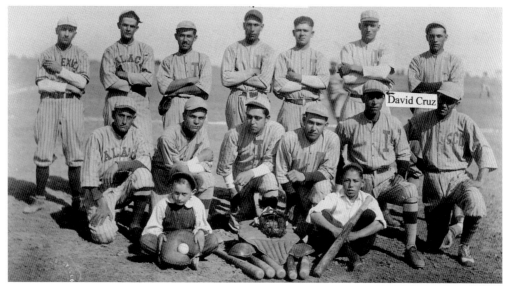

Mexican Americans from the San Fernando Valley traveled to join teams from different regions of Southern California. Posing here with the Calexico club in Imperial County are infielder David Cruz (second row, second from right) and pitcher Cecil Cruz (third row, fourth from left). David and Cecil made up two of the four Cruz brothers who hailed from San Fernando and played on the San Fernando Merchants. They also played for other Valley teams as substitutes. (Courtesy of Alice Cruz Bacon and Theresa Alicia Bacon.)

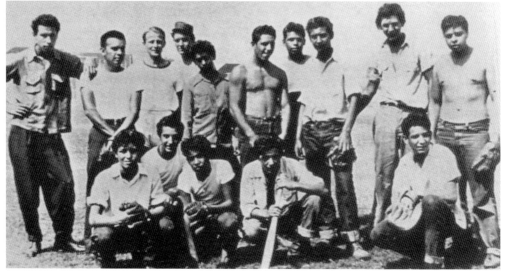

The players on the Burbank Holy Trinity Parish team are, from left to right, (first row) Cirilo Gonzáles, David García, Bob Santoyo, Richard Ruiz, and Fred Saenz; (second row) Ernie Vásquez, Steve Ríos, unidentified, Ralph Gallegos, Albert Duron, Frank Lara, Tony Hernández, J.D. García, Frank Doris, and Robert Barrera. Holy Trinity Parish, now known as St. Robert Bellarmine, was one of the earliest Catholic churches in the San Fernando Valley, serving Burbank and Sun Valley. (Courtesy of Alex Saenz and Ramona Valenzuela Cervantes.)

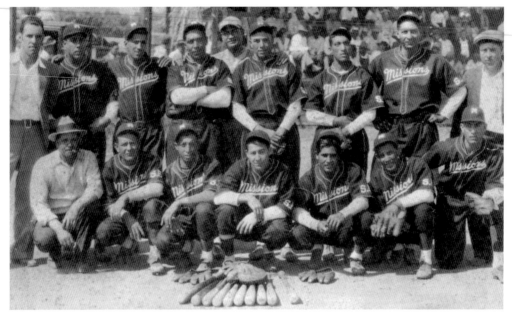

The 1930s Missions, the preeminent Mexican American semipro team in San Fernando, is seen at White Sox Park in Los Angeles. The team included manager Juan Durazo (first row, far left), John García (first row, third from left), Robert Uribe (first row, second from right), and Chris García (second row, third from right). The Missions traveled throughout California and Mexico, playing in Tijuana and Mexicali. The team further maintained transnational connections, as Mexican teams visited San Fernando from Tijuana to Sinaloa. The Missions uniforms were imported from Mexico.

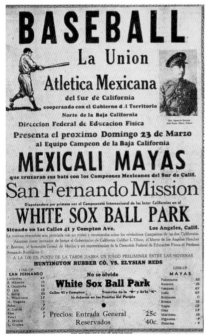

This 1939 poster advertises a playoff matchup, organized by the Mexican Athletic Union, between the Baja California champions (Mexicali Mayas) and the Southern California Mexican champions (San Fernando Missions) for the Inter-Californias International championship. Special attendees included California governor Culbert L. Olson, Los Angeles mayor Fletcher Bowron, and the consul of Mexico, Prof. Armando Rodriguez, representing the Mexican Federal Office of Physical Education. (Courtesy of Chris García Jr.)

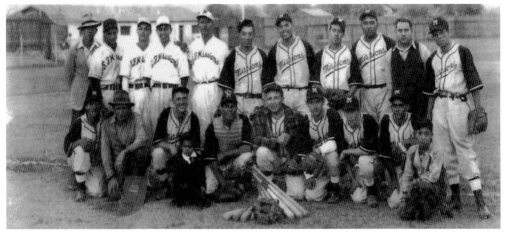

A 1940s Missions team gathers at San Fernando Park. Shown here are, from left to right, (first row) Chris García, Chief Herrera, two unidentified persons, Tony Méndez, Lupe Villanueva, Robert Uribe, and Angel Guajardo; (second row) unidentified, Rudy Flores, Félix Bustamante, Frank Parra, Leo Guerra, John García, Nick Salas, Joe García, Marin Magana, umpire Chapo Yidal, and Ray Serra; batboy David García is kneeling at far right; the other boy is unidentified. Herrera, a pool hall owner in San Fernando, was a sponsor of the Missions. (Courtesy of Chris García Jr.)

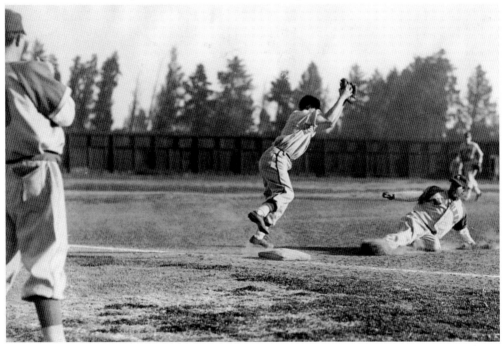

Chris García of the Missions slides safely into third base at San Fernando Park. This park was the premier baseball field in the San Fernando Valley throughout the 1940s and 1950s and the onetime spring-training home of the Seattle Rainiers and Hollywood Stars. Connie Mack and the Philadelphia Athletics frequently visited in the preseason, attracting up to 5,000 spectators. The park included a clubhouse with showers and a locker room. (Courtesy of Chris García Jr.)

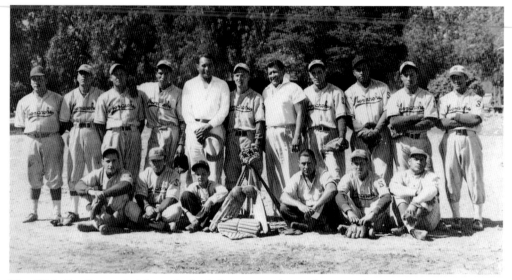

The 1930s San Fernando Monarchs had players interchange between the Missions and Monarchs. Shown here are, from left to right, (first row) Joe Ponce, unidentified, Félix Bustamante, umpire Chapo Yidal, Robert Uribe, and Elijio Salas; (second row) two unidentified players, Joe Miranda, Ernie Rios, manager Arturo Magana, Frankie Pérez, unidentified, Jess Franco, Marin Magana, John García, and Chris García. Joe Ponce was the trainer of Bobby Chacon from Pacoima, who won boxing titles and is a member of the International Boxing Hall of Fame. (Courtesy of Chris García Jr.)

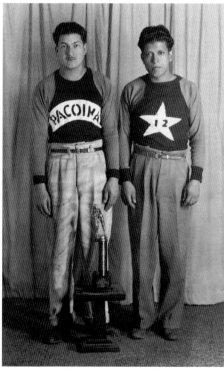

Lupe G. Hernández (right), one of the best players in the San Fernando Valley, was born in Amarillo, Texas, in 1914. He moved to Pacoima at age five and spent the remainder of his life there. Lupe hung around fields, hoping to play. A talented catcher, he played for decades before coaching his grandchildren's teams. Terry Hernández recalls being with her siblings, watching her dad play: "He loved baseball; it was a part of him." (Courtesy of Terry Hernández and Rita Hernández Ontiveros.)

The 1947 Pacoima team featured, from left to right, (first row) Lupe Hernández, George Villanueva, Pete Prieto, Benny Salas, and Pete Almada; (second row) Poncho Torres, Angel Luna, Nacho Calzada, Eddie Prieto, Ted Villanueva, and Del Rey. Teams played at Pacoima Park, now David M. Gonzáles Recreation Center. The Prieto brothers, Eddie and Pete, were the force behind Pacoima teams for years. Eddie became a California highway patrolman, and Pete worked as a Los Angeles police officer and detective. (Courtesy of Joe García Jr.)

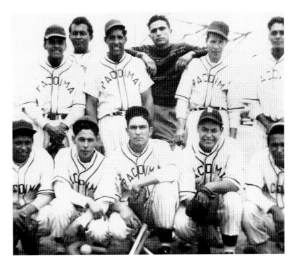

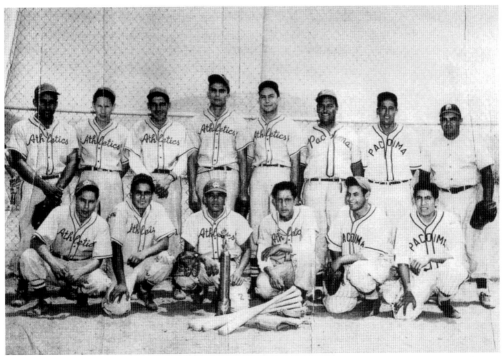

The Pacoima Athletic Club poses with its Municipal League award at Pacoima Park. Shown here are, from left to right, (first row) George Villanueva, Del Rey, Poncho Torres, Ray Cuellar, Benny Salas, and Frank Salas; (second row) Nacho Calzada, Ted Villanueva, Manuel Gonzáles, Eddie Prieto, Pete Prieto, Percy Ramírez, Simon Salas, and Joffee García. Most players lived in the barrio of Pacoima, east of the tracks along San Fernando Road up to Glenoaks Boulevard. (Courtesy of Joe García Jr.)

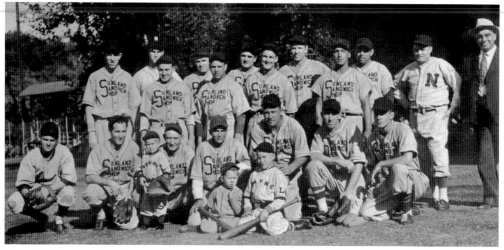

The 1941 Sunland Sandwich Shop team included Chris García (third row, far right), George Vico (fourth row, second from left), and Nick Salas (fourth row, third from right). Yugoslav American George Vico played on the Naval team in San Diego. In 1948, he made his debut for the Detroit Tigers and became one of the rare players to hit a home run on the first pitch he saw. He later played for the Hollywood Stars and San Francisco Seals in the Pacific Coast League. (Courtesy of Chris García Jr.)

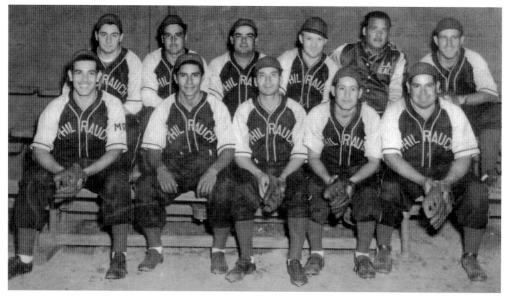

The Phil Rauch Studebaker dealership in Burbank sponsored a team. Shown here are, from left to right, (first row) Gene Madrid, John De La Cerda, unidentified, Bill Alba, and Vince Salas; (second row) two unidentified players, Joffee García, and three unidentified players. Mexican American families often had multiple players on teams. Bill Alba's brother Mike played alongside Jackie Robinson on the Pasadena Junior College team in the late 1930s. His other brothers Sipriano, Bob, and Kinteen played for San Fernando and Simi Valley teams, while brothers Pete, Danny, and Andy Alba played in Pacoima.

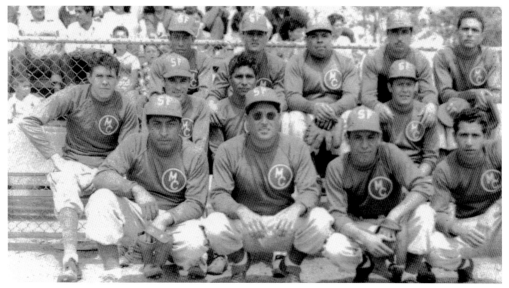

Martínez Café, a popular bar and restaurant, sponsored softball teams. Posing here are, from left to right, (first row) David Vaiz, Federico Carmona, Frank Parra, and John Alcantar; (second row) two unidentified, John De La Cerda, and Bill Alba; (third row) Alex Vaiz, Félix Bustamante, Vince Salas, Rod Rodríguez, and Eddie Prieto. Other members of the Vaiz family included brothers Mike, Paul, and Harold, who played in softball and Catholic Youth Organization leagues, and sister Isabelle, who played for the Blue Jays.

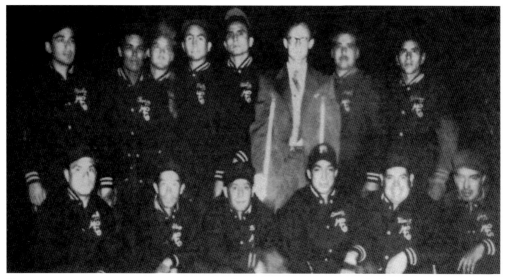

Various construction companies sponsored Mexican American softball teams. The Malcolm Paving softball team of San Fernando included, from left to right, (first row) unidentified, Alex Vaiz, Bill Alba, David García, Vince Salas, and unidentified; (second row) Rudy Aragón, Ray Barraza, Felix Bustamante, Pete Prieto, Eddie Prieto, ? Malcolm, Angel Rodríguez, and John De La Cerda. Throughout the 1950s, Malcolm Paving was among the top Triple-A softball teams in the Valley, annually competing in championship games. (Courtesy of Joe García Jr.)

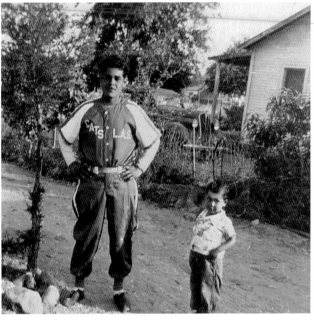

Known as the "King of the Home Run," Marcos Castillo played for the Classy Cats team of San Fernando in the late 1940s. A former military ballplayer in World War II, Castillo is seen here in 1947 with son Marcos Castillo Jr. The photograph was taken around La Rue Street and Laurel Canyon Boulevard, near the current San Fernando High School. The San Fernando High Tigers won the Los Angeles City Section Division I baseball titles in 2011 and 2013. (Courtesy of Ramona Valenzuela Cervantes.)

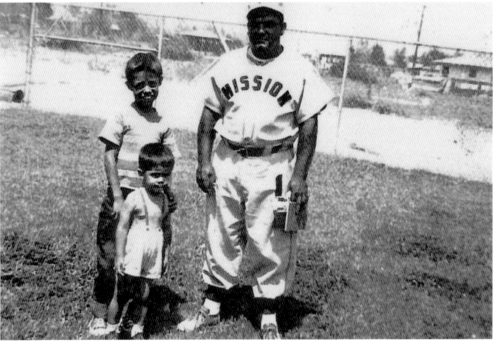

Joffee García stands with sons Joe Jr. (left) and John in 1953 at Pacoima Park. Games were family outings, complete with barbeques and festivities. Players brought their families along when they played in other regions. Joe Jr. remembers his family taking weekend camping trips to Santa Barbara and Santa Maria, where his dad played on Sundays. Joe Jr. followed in his father's footsteps, playing for the Valley Merchants in the 1960s and Polytechnic High School in Sun Valley. (Courtesy of Joe García Jr.)

SAN FERNANDO VALLEY

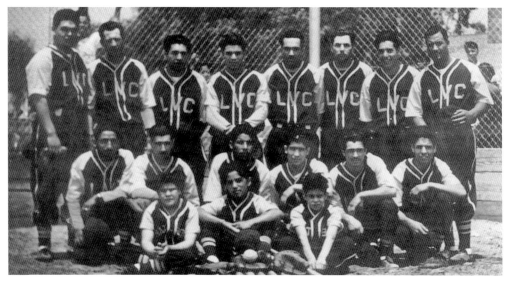

The Lankershim Village Club (LVC) originated in the Orcasitas barrio of North Hollywood. Posing in the early 1940s are, from left to right, (first row) Rudy Madrid, Victor Ramírez, and Alfred Moreno; (second row) Ysabel Ramírez, David Alderete, Thomas Díaz, William Moreno, Mike Alderete, and Tony Velarde; (third row) Mark Montoya, Bill Chávez, Joe Pérez, Alfred Márquez, Tony Servera, Dan Padilla, Vince Sánchez, and manager Percy Ramírez. Many of the players were veterans of World War II. (Courtesy of Mike Velarde.)

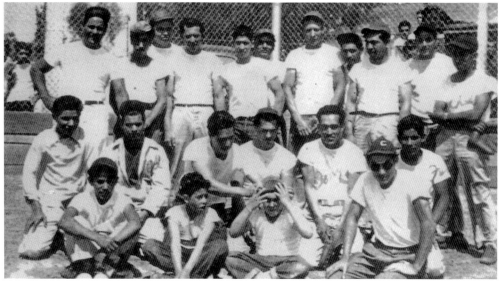

Shown on this 1940s Orcasitas neighborhood team are, from left to right, (first row) Victor Ramírez, Alfred Moreno, Rudy Madrid, and Manuel Ybarra; (second row) Manuel Díaz, Al Márquez, Vince Sánchez, Mike Alderete, Tony Servera, and Thomas Díaz; (third row) Percy Ramírez, John Perez, Mark Montoya, Bill Chávez, Willie Moreno, Joffee García, Alex Chávez, David Alderete, unidentified, Danny Padilla, and Ysabel Ramírez. Ybarra ran a waste-management company, and Servera founded a concrete contracting business, now in its third generation. (Courtesy of Mike Velarde.)

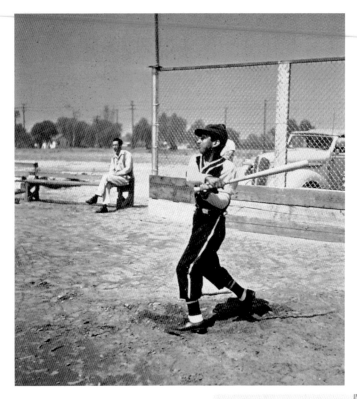

Ysabel Ramírez takes a swing at the neighborhood ball field on Stagg Street and Irvine Avenue. Ramírez was a talented player for the Lankershim Village Club in the Orcasitas barrio of North Hollywood. Like most Mexican American players at the time, he served in the military, joining the Army in August 1945. He was stationed in Luzon, Philippines, and received the Asiatic-Pacific ribbon. Ramírez stayed active in softball, later coaching the North Hollywood Vixies women's club. (Courtesy of Mike Ramírez.)

Joffee García (left), seen here at San Fernando Park in 1947 with the Missions, was a talented and well-traveled catcher for many years in the San Fernando Valley. Raised in Pacoima, García attended San Fernando High School. He played for countless semipro baseball and softball clubs throughout the Valley in Pacoima, San Fernando, Burbank, North Hollywood, Sunland, and Canoga Park. On occasion, he played for teams in other regions, such as the Monrovia Merchants. (Courtesy of Joe García Jr.)

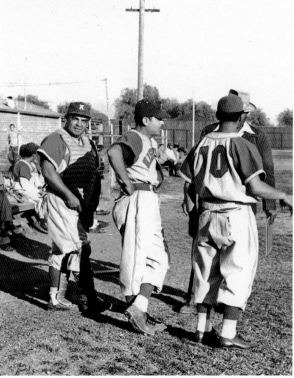

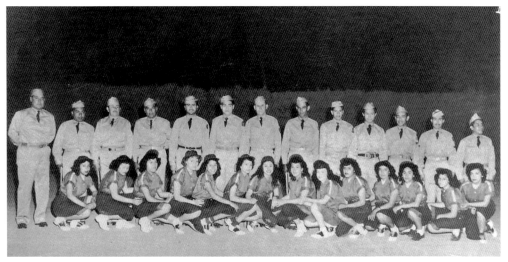

The San Fernando Blue Jays were champions of the Valley women's softball league in 1948. The team is seen here in 1949 at Las Palmas Park with sponsors Woodmen of the World insurance. Members of the Blue Jays are, from left to right, Josephine Vaiz, Virginia Tapia, Cecilia Morales, unidentified, Isabelle Vaiz, Rosie Imperial, Candy Solís, Tonie Imperial, Rosie Perez, Jennie Vaiz, Licha Garcia, Gloria Palafox, Josephine Morales, and Constance Espinosa. Spectacular players included shortstop Vaiz and the Imperial sisters, pitcher Rosie and catcher Tonie. (Courtesy of Isabelle Vaiz Mejia.)

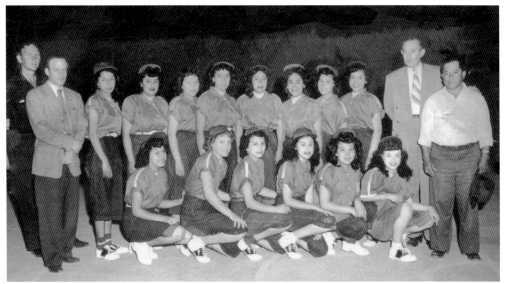

This photograph of the San Fernando Blue Jays includes Isabelle Vaiz (second row, third from left) and brother Pete Vaiz (standing, far right). Pete served as manager and provided team transportation, using the truck in which he hauled Blue Goose–brand oranges for the American Fruit Growers Corporation. Most of the Blue Jays attended San Fernando High School. The team's uniform consisted of pedal pushers with blouses provided by Woodmen of the World. (Courtesy of Isabelle Vaiz Mejia.)

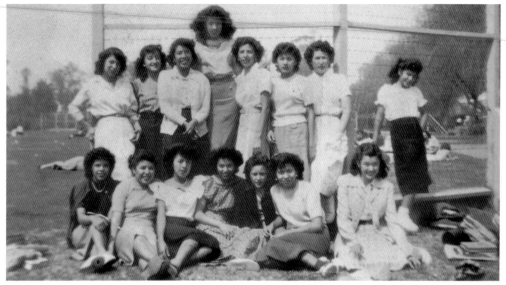

Seen here at the North Hollywood High School baseball field in 1949 are members of the Vixies, a softball team. They are, from left to right, (first row) Flora Ortiz, Rosie Chávez, Ramona Valenzuela, Teresa Hernández, unidentified, Rita Chávez, and unidentified; (second row) Jennie Duran, Jennie Chacon, Carmen Salas, Julia Salazar, Jennie Coranado, Estella Quijada, Lupe Montenegro, and unidentified. Pitcher Valenzuela and catcher Quijada were members of the GAA Lettergirl's Club. (Courtesy of Ramona Valenzuela Cervantes.)

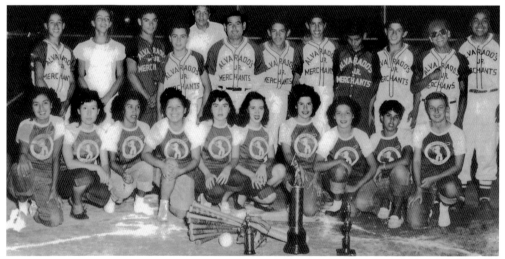

Posing in the front row are members of the Burbank B Bops. They are, from left to right, Ramona Sarmiento, Margaret Escudero, Eleanor Yanez, Lupe Díaz, Tencha Moreno, Margaret Moreno, unidentified, Marie Alvarado, Judy Davila, and Jean Snyder. The 1950 Burbank boys' park league champions, the Alvarado Jr. Merchants, stand in the second row. They are, from left to right, Eddie Orduñez, Héctor Carbajal, Mike Velarde, Paul Ramírez, Moe Montanez, Hank Alvarado, John Lara, Carlos Dávila, George Alvarado, David Fernández, Manuel Díaz, and Charlie Gameros. (Courtesy of Alex Sáenz and Ramona Valenzuela Cervantes.)

Rudy Aragón was a gifted player from the San Fernando Valley. A four-year letterman at San Fernando High, he made the All–San Fernando Valley team every year. In 1949, he made the all-city team as shortstop. Aragón lettered in football and excelled on the last softball team in 1946. He played in the Baltimore Orioles farm system for the Riverside Rubes and played softball for Martínez Café, Malcolm Paving, and Del Rey Paving. (Courtesy of Rudy Aragón and Tommy Tapia.)

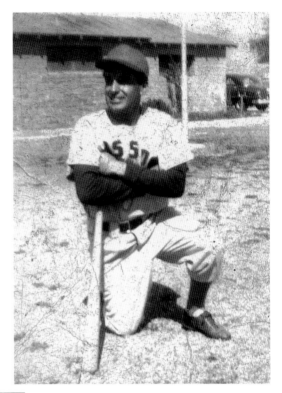

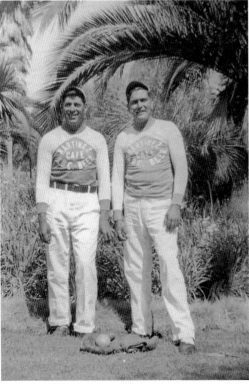

Seen here are Martínez Café softball teammates and close friends Nick Salas (left) and Rubén Ruiz. First baseman Ruiz played on various baseball clubs. He worked as a truck driver for the San Fernando citrus packinghouses, processing crops from the nearby orchards. Hard-hitting third basemen Salas was one of the most revered Mexican American players in the San Fernando Valley and a stalwart for the San Fernando Missions. (Courtesy of Everto Ruiz.)

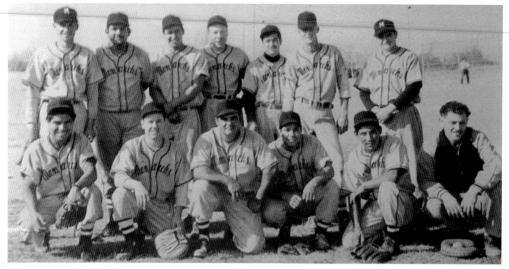

Members of the Valley Monarchs are, from left to right, (first row) Manuel Díaz, unidentified, Joffee García, Wally García, Tom Díaz, and Angel Alvarado; (second row) Billy Chávez, Sonny Padilla, Frank Vela, Alex Chavez, Mike Alderete, unidentified, and Jimmy Madrid. This team played at Fernangeles Park in Sun Valley and traveled to Camarillo, Oxnard, Santa Barbara, and Santa Maria. The Monarchs faced Van Nuys pitcher Don Drysdale, who later pitched for the Los Angeles Dodgers. The team won the 1962–1963 Municipal Winter Park League championship. (Courtesy of Joe García Jr.)

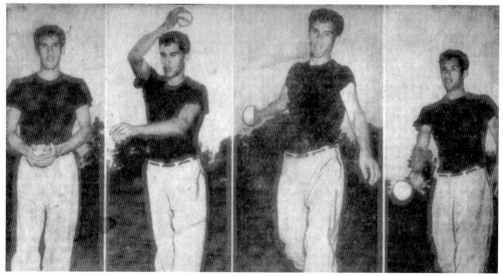

Ray Barraza was the best fast-pitch softball pitcher in the San Fernando Valley during the 1950s. Known as the "Buzzbomb" by the *Van Nuys News and Valley Green Sheet*, Barraza grew up in Van Nuys pitching for Malcolm Paving. He made the All-Star Valley team, played for city championships, and won the top pitcher award from the Major Softball Association. In 1954, he broke the Major Softball Association record for strikeouts in a season, compiling an incredible 212. (Courtesy of Daniel and Mark Barraza.)

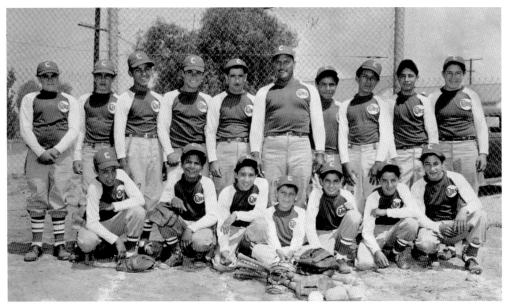

The 1952 North Hollywood Cubs pose for a team photograph. Shown here are, from left to right, (first row) Freddie Martínez, Charlie Díaz, Dickie Beltrán, Joe Padilla (batboy), Tommy Chávez, Manuel Valenzuela, and Rudy Beltrán; (second row) Rudy Madrid, Alfred Moreno, Victor Ramírez, Tony Velarde, David Alderete, Percy Ramírez (coach), Manuel Díaz, Joey Díaz, Tony Castillo, and Ray González. Percy managed in North Hollywood and Pacoima. Born in New Mexico in 1907, he moved to North Hollywood, served during World War II, and later worked in construction. (Courtesy of Mike Velarde.)

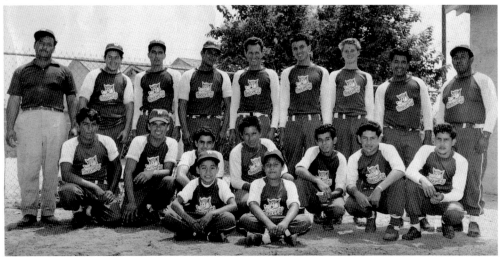

The Wolves formed in the Orcasitas barrio of North Hollywood. This 1950s team includes, from left to right, (first row) Anthony Servera Jr. and Frank Castillo; (second row) Victor Ramírez, Tony Velarde, Tommy Chávez, Joey Díaz, George Alvarado, John Lara, and Alfred Moreno; (third row) Percy Ramírez, Ray González, unidentified, Chris Sánchez, Bill Chávez, Aurelio Enciso, Wesley ? , ? Reyes, and Inez Reyes. (Courtesy of Mike Velarde.)

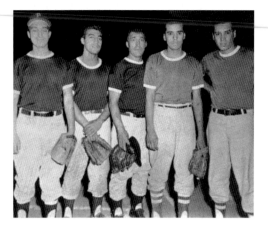

Participating in Old Timers Day at San Fernando Park in 1962 are, from left to right, David García, Chris García Jr., Chris García Sr., Joey García, and John García Jr. Chris Sr. tried out with the Los Angeles Angels (of the PCL) and played in the Mexican League, while David tried out for the Hollywood Stars. Chris, John, and Joe played for the Missions, and sister Licha played for the Blue Jays. Joe served during World War II, and David and Chris Jr. served in Korea. (Courtesy of Chris García Jr.)

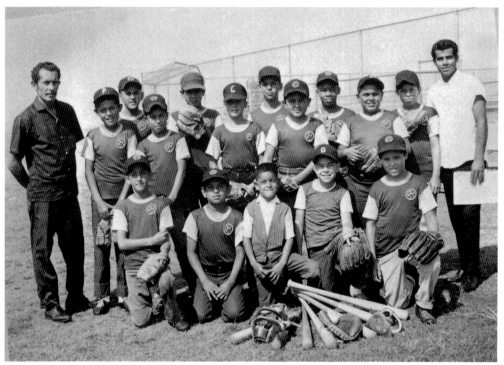

This team from Pacoima, sponsored by 7-Up, poses in Paxton Park in 1964. Shown here are, from left to right, (first row) unidentified, Ronnie Puga, two unidentified players, and Johnny Contreras; (second row) manager Joseph Cervantes, Manuel Cervantes, Gus García, two unidentified players, Anthony Duarte, unidentified, Delfino López, Albert Green, Joey Cervantes, Johnny Hernández, and unidentified. Joseph Cervantes coached Little, Pony, and Park Leagues in Arleta, Pacoima, San Fernando, and Lake View Terrace. He won the 1977 Manager of the Year award while coaching the Valley Saints. (Courtesy of Ramona Valenzuela Cervantes.)

SAN FERNANDO VALLEY

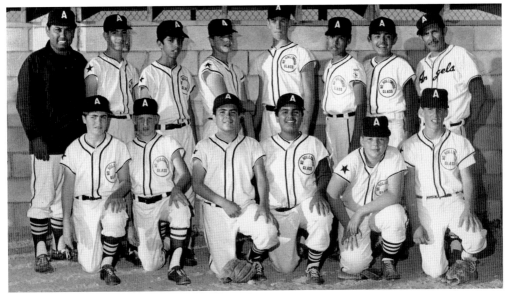

The 1969 Arleta Angels team included Joey Cervantes (first row, third from right), Manuel Cervantes (second row, second from right), and their father, coach Joseph Cervantes (second row, far right). The team was sponsored by North Hollywood Glass. Since the 1950s, Mexican American youths increasingly participated in Little, Babe Ruth, and Pony Leagues, as well as American Legion baseball, marking a shift from earlier independent community teams. (Courtesy of Ramona Valenzuela Cervantes.)

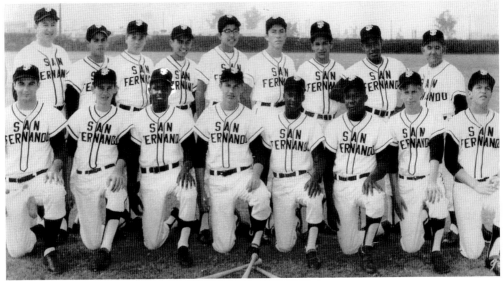

The 1970 San Fernando High School team included Robert Corrales (second row, fifth from left) and Anthony Davis (second row, second from right), who later played running back for USC. Corrales made the 1970 All-City Team and was drafted by the Houston Astros. He played for College of the Canyons, helping the team win the 1973 Western State Conference title. He also played for Pepperdine University and the Tijuana Potros (Colts) in the Mexican League. In 2013, he was inducted into the College of the Canyons Sports Hall of Fame. (Courtesy of Rudy Corrales.)

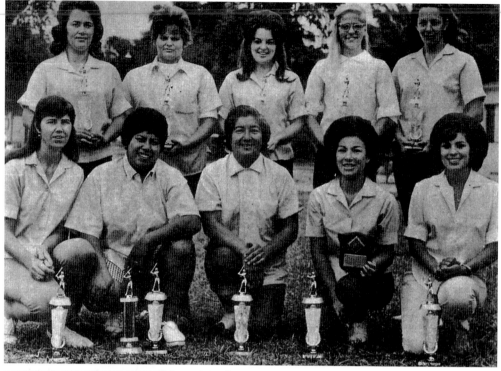

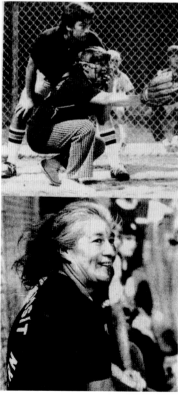

Members of the Sylmar Las Muñecas (The Dolls) women's softball team proudly display their championship trophies as winners of the 1969 Sylmar Park Softball League. They are, from left to right, (first row) Wanda Green, Terry Hernández, Epimenia Delgado, Carmen Orduna, and Anna Aguilar; (second row) Angie Avalos, Peggy Stockton, Carol Morris, Vicki Dresser, and Pat Ziegler. Pitcher Terry Hernández won the Outstanding Player award. The women played on traveling teams, visiting Sunland, Sun Valley, and Canoga Park. (Courtesy of Terry Hernández and Rita Delgado.)

Epimenia Delgado was a renowned player in the San Fernando Valley. Born and raised in San Fernando, she got involved with softball in her mid-forties, playing for women's and coed leagues in Sylmar, San Fernando, Sun Valley, and Canyon Country. Her daughter Rita remembered that "playing softball was her joy and passion in life. This made her a happy woman. This was her outlet from being a busy mother and wife." Delgado collected 30 trophies throughout her softball career. (Courtesy of Rita Delgado.)

SAN FERNANDO VALLEY

2

VENTURA COUNTY

Beautiful Ventura County has always beckoned as a place to build a new life. Fr. Junipero Serra founded a mission in the city of San Buenaventura in 1782. The Californios built ranchos in the surrounding area during the mid-1800s. The Mexican Revolution of 1910 brought a huge influx of Mexicans to California, with many settling here. Jobs were plentiful in the burgeoning agriculture industry. In the early 1900s, sugar beet and lima bean fields dotted the county, as did fruit orchards. Later, the citrus industry took over, and jobs picking oranges and lemons or working in the packinghouses were abundant.

Although Mexicans have inhabited the region for 200 years, they have always faced discrimination as outsiders. Most Mexican families lived in barrios, segregated Mexican neighborhoods located in undesirable areas of town; however, these barrios created a sense of community, fostered by activities and the church. Families joined *mutualistas*, fraternal organizations that provided support in times of need. And, in their leisure hours, many men turned to baseball, a sport they had played in Mexico. Baseball has existed in Ventura County since the late 1800s.

When the braceros (Mexican contract laborers) arrived in Ventura County in the 1940s, discrimination intensified. Businesses, theaters, and even churches were segregated. Many of the braceros played baseball, but only in camps. The sport was a way to build unity, strengthen friendships, hone skills, and to forget, for nine innings, that they were different. It became a source of pride for the players as well as the residents of the barrio and, ultimately, was a great equalizer. The men who worked in the packinghouses worked alongside Anglo workers. It seemed natural for them to invite coworkers to play on their teams. Soon, players of different ethnicities were working and playing together.

The four-year-old grandson of one of this book's authors, Anna Bermúdez, played his first baseball game. He is a lefty with attitude! After the game, Justin was asked why he chose to forego T-ball and go straight to baseball. He had watched this chapter being created; he had seen the photographs. "My uncles did it," he said.

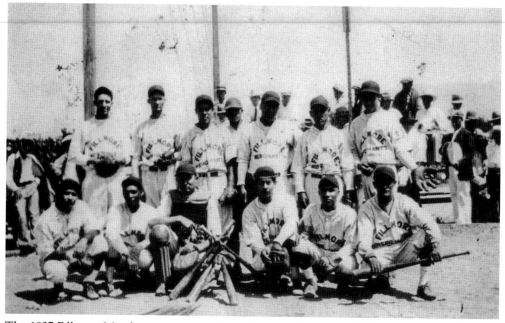

The 1927 Fillmore Merchants are seen after a winning day on the field. The Merchants played around Ventura County, traveling up to Santa Barbara and down to Los Angeles. Their reputation provided them with opportunities to play outside of Southern California. The Merchants often traveled on weekends to Tijuana to play Mexican teams. Shown here are, from left to right, (first row) Dolores Sánchez, unidentified, Francisco Chaveste, unidentified, Arnulfo Sánchez, and unidentified; (second row) two unidentified players, Jesus López, and three unidentified players. (Courtesy of the Sánchez family.)

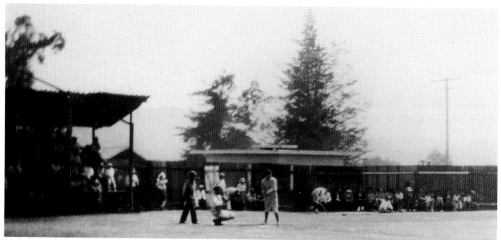

In 1928, the Fillmore baseball field was located on Ventura Street between Clay and Saratoga Streets (now Highway 126). The barrio in Fillmore was divided by railroad tracks. Barrio Santo was the scene of Mexican religious celebrations, such as Las Posadas and La Pastorela. The Barrio de Las Flores was known for its beautiful gardens. The location of the ball field was ideal for families since it was a short walk to the southern end of Barrio Santo. (Courtesy of the Sánchez family.)

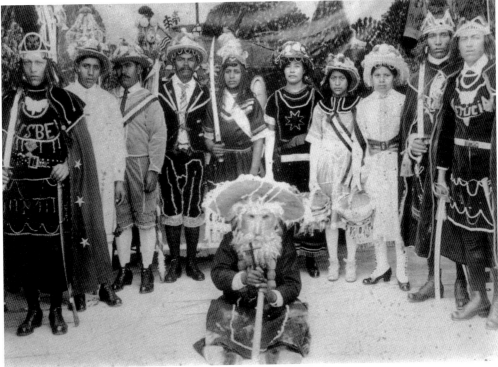

The Mexican community celebrated the 16th of September event as its feast of independence, and, during the Christmas season, it gathered to participate in Las Posadas and La Pastorela, a medieval shepherd's play. In 1916, a group of residents from Fillmore pose in costume for La Pastorela. All of the men worked in the agriculture industry. Shown here are, standing from left to right, Crispín Rivas, Carlos Sánchez, Lorenzo Sánchez, Hipólito Rodríguez, Dolores Sánchez, Maria Hinojosa, Ventura Rivas, Narcisa Rivas, Guadalupe Hinojosa, and Manuel Rivas; Florentino Muñoz is seated in front. (Courtesy of the Sánchez family.)

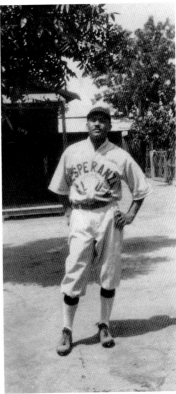

While a member of the Fillmore Merchants, Dolores Sánchez played with Club Esperanza in Fillmore. This photograph was taken on Clay Street, adjacent to the ball field, on May 5, 1927. Club Esperanza was a sports club affiliated with the mutualistas, community-based mutual-aid societies popular in barrios of the Southwest. They provided a safe haven and refuge against discrimination. Many provided health and burial insurance and served as social clubs with planned cultural activities. (Courtesy of the Sánchez family.)

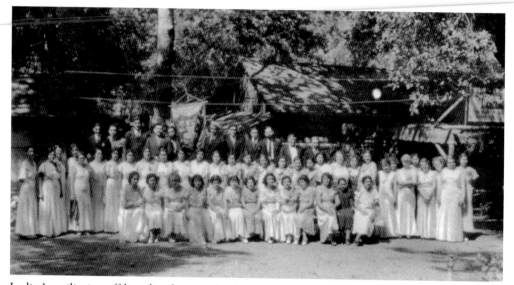

Ladies' auxiliaries, affiliated with mutual-aid organizations, planned activities, including picnics and costume parties as well as celebrations during Cinco de Mayo and Mexican Independence Day. Spanish grammar was taught to children after school or on Saturdays by former teachers, and music lessons were offered. The Campamento Benito Juárez Sociedad Mutualista meeting in Steckel Park in Santa Paula, seen here in 1930, was a social event planned by the women's auxiliary. *Campamento* means "camp" in English. (Courtesy of the Flores family.)

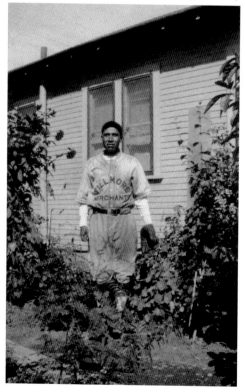

Arnulfo Sánchez stands on the side yard of the Sánchez family home on Santa Clara Street in Fillmore in 1930. His two brothers, Arnulfo and Dolores, played ball. The Sánchez family arrived from Guanajuato, Mexico, in 1906. Their father, Abundio Sánchez, worked on the railroad in Texas and Kansas. He came to Fillmore in 1912 to work in agriculture. By 1919, Abundio Sánchez and his sons had saved money to build their own business, Sánchez Brothers Mexican Mercantile. (Courtesy of the Sánchez family.)

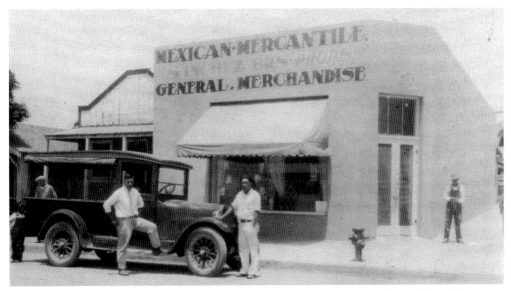

Carlos and Arnulfo Sánchez pose in 1923 in front of the Mexican Mercantile store located on Main and Mountain View Streets in Fillmore. The store was run by Abundio's sons: Carlos, Arnulfo, and Dolores. The basement became a site for dances, wedding receptions, and meetings. The Sánchez brothers lost the store during the Depression, as their father could never turn anyone away for lack of money. The González family purchased the store, operating it until the Northridge earthquake of 1994. (Courtesy of the Sánchez family.)

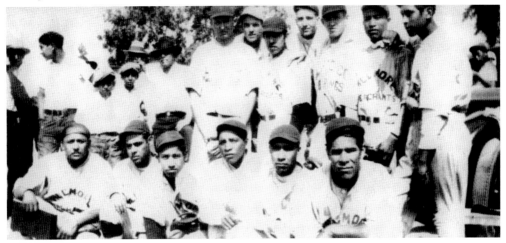

In 1931, the Fillmore Merchants ball club was comprised of players who worked in the citrus industry. Among the Mexican players were Anglos. Ernie Morales, son of pitcher Frank Morales, said that his father attributed it to the fact they worked alongside each other. It was a natural transition to ask them to join the team. The Merchants had a reputation as a top club in Southern California. Pictured from left to right are (first row) Dolores Sánchez (catcher), Mecho Muñoz, Frank Morales (pitcher), Dionisio Espinoza, Arnulfo Sánchez, and Jesús López; (second row) Waldo Parrish, unidentified, Tom Martines, unidentified, Roy Imhoff, Ignacio Garnica, and Joaquín Sauceda. (Courtesy of Ernie Morales.)

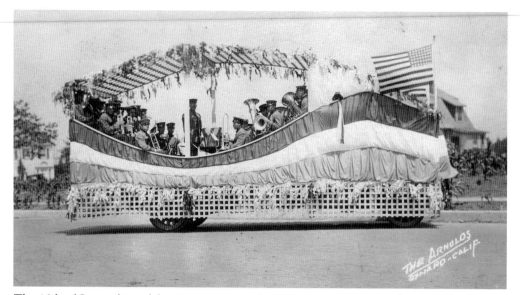

The 16th of September celebration was a time for Mexican Americans to honor and reflect on the country they had left behind. The Fillmore Citrus Association's manager, Frank Erskine, organized a Mexican band. Led by conductor and music teacher Manuel Lucero, the band was popular with the community of Fillmore and was available for any occasion. This decorated float was for the 16th of September celebration in Oxnard in 1927. The band's motto was, "Money spent for music is a sound investment." (Courtesy of the Flores family.)

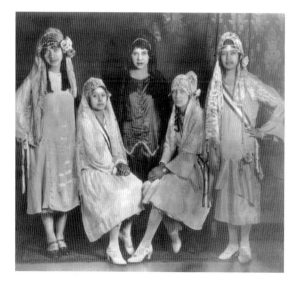

Cinco de Mayo was celebrated in the barrios of Ventura County. Although not as important as Mexican Independence Day, the day was still a cause for residents of the barrio to gather for parades and festivities. Floats were designed and decorated by various organizations, activities were organized, food was offered, and a contest for Cinco de Mayo queen was held. This photograph shows the queen and her court of the Cinco de Mayo parade in 1921. Second from the left is Refugio Sánchez, and third from the left is Lupe Sandoval. (Courtesy of Ofelia Haynes.)

Woody Ybarra spent many hours at his grandparents' home on Santa Clara Street, where he is pictured here. Woody was the son of Soledad Sánchez Ybarra and Aurelio Ybarra. Woody had a great baseball mind. He played in high school and pitched for the Fillmore Merchants long after his uncles hung up their gloves. He also played ball in the military during World War II. Born Marcelino Ybarra, he was given the nickname of "Woody" because of his amazing athletic ability. Harry Bigger, Fillmore High School principal, said Woody was the finest pitcher he had ever seen, but Mexicans were not considered for major-league ball. He took Woody to a Dodger-Yankees baseball game in Los Angeles, and he was able to meet Mickey Mantle, a memory that neither Bigger nor Woody would ever forget. (Courtesy of Ybarra family.)

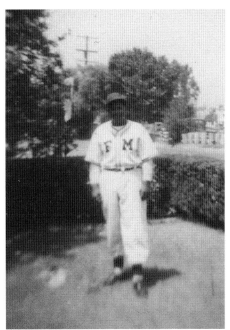

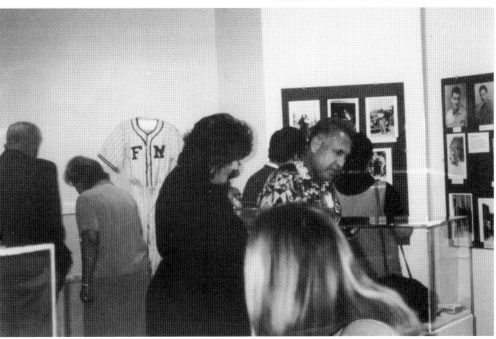

In 1999, the Museum of Ventura County presented an exhibition on the history of the Mexican American community in Ventura County. The exhibit attracted an ethnic demographic to the museum that had rarely visited there before: Mexican Americans. Artifacts and stories were collected from all communities in the county. Among the objects was the Fillmore Merchants baseball uniform worn by Woody Ybarra (seen in the background). (Courtesy of Museum of Ventura County.)

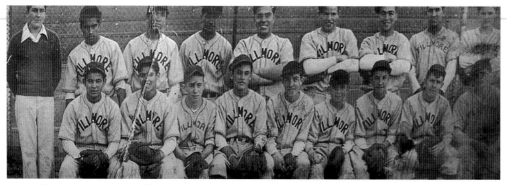

The Fillmore Merchants ball club was still going strong after World War II. This 1945 photograph shows that the majority of the athletes were Mexican. Second baseman Robert Muñoz is in the first row, fourth from left, and Pete Carrillo is second from left. (Courtesy of Alex Muñoz.)

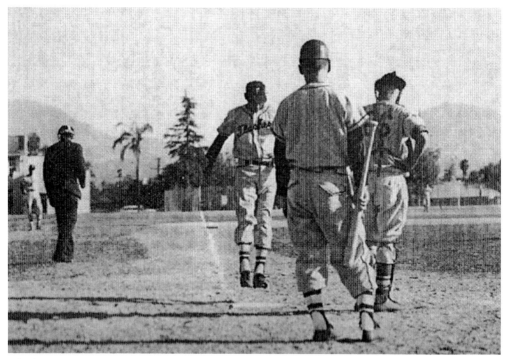

Ed Ybarra followed his brother Woody and played with the Fillmore Little League program, and brother Lou played in the outfield. At Fillmore High School, Ed played pitcher and shortstop. This photograph of Ed (center) was taken in 1962. The school team, the Flashes, included ? Tovar, Art Medina, Tony Cervantez, and Frank Ibarra. Ed was scouted by the Los Angeles Angels. He played in the adult league in Piru, coached Little League, and played in the senior league in Pennsylvania. (Courtesy of Ed Ybarra.)

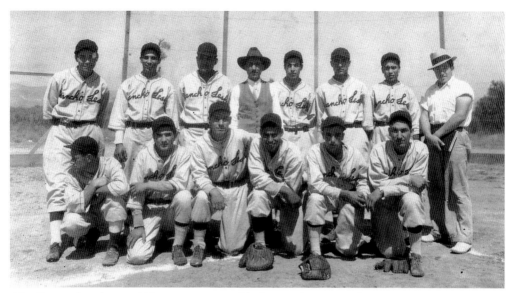

Alex Davis played on a 1930s team sponsored by his employer, Rancho Sespe, a citrus business in Ventura County west of Fillmore. Shown here are, from left to right, (first row) two unidentified players, ? Cota, Henry Ibarra, ? Carrillo, and Gilbert Ozuna; (second row) unidentified, John Castoreña, Alex Davis, Catarino ? (manager), Chavelo Sánchez, Primitivo Calles, Henry García, and David Cervantez. (Courtesy of Sandra Davis Gunderson.)

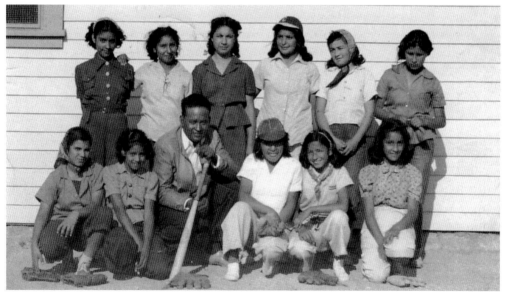

Alex Davis coached this team of women. Of special note is the player standing to the far left, Carmen Dolores Vásquez Ramírez. Years later, Davis would explain that he always had her playing right field because fewer balls were hit to that spot. This kept the error-prone player from handling the ball too much. Davis and Carmen were married for 57 years. They had three children—Carlos, Adrian and Sandi—and enjoyed baseball as their children grew up. (Courtesy of Sandra Davis Gunderson.)

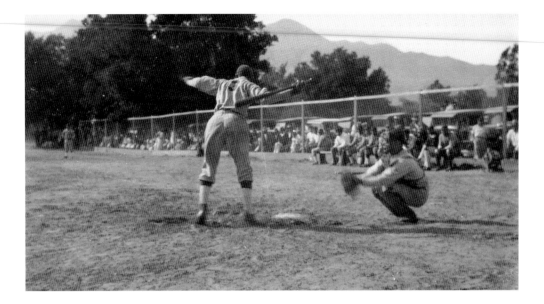

With the silhouette of the San Cayetano Mountain summit in the background, the Rancho Sespe team plays while spectators look on (above). The informality of the setting allowed fans a close-up view of every play, including this inside pitch that the agile batter springs back to avoid. The stinging slap of the ball in the catcher's mitt may still be hanging in the air. Alex Davis and Carmen Ramírez enjoyed watching a good game (below), whether it was played by a family member or the Los Angeles Dodgers, their favorite team since it drafted Jackie Robinson in the 1940s. If there were a hall of fame for love stories that began on a baseball diamond, the one between Alex and Carmen would have a place of honor. (Courtesy of Sandra Davis Gunderson.)

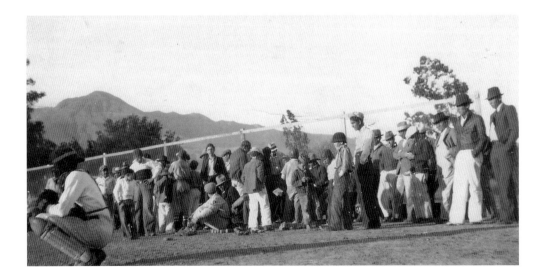

VENTURA COUNTY

The communities of Fillmore and Santa Paula are located along the Santa Clara River. In the early 1900s, the predominant crops were lima beans and walnuts. Later years saw the development of the citrus industry. This 1917 photograph was taken near Bardsdale, an unincorporated area outside of Fillmore. (Courtesy of Irene Gonzalez.)

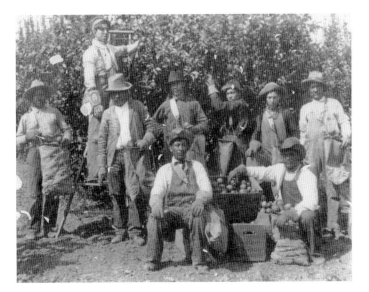

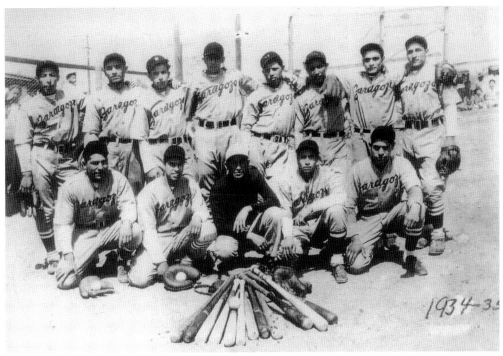

The 1930s Santa Paula Zaragoza ball club was comprised of players working for the Teague-McKevett Citrus Association. Players came from other cities or clubs to play in Santa Paula. Rufino Cuevas came from Santa Barbara, while the Maestas brothers, Raul and Ralph, traveled from Los Angeles for the games. Shown here are, from left to right, (first row) Jesús Ramírez, Tolin Ramos, Raúl Maestas, Ralph Maestas, and Rufino Cuevas; (second row) Minnie Cobos, Paul Coronado, Max ?, three unidentified persons, Pete Hughes, and Toby ?.

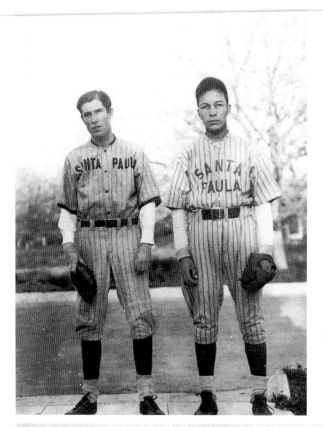

The Santa Paula Merchants ball club was formed in a small community about 14 miles east of Ventura in the geographical center of the county. The Merchants (below) played on a ball field located at Twelfth and Santa Paula Streets in the barrio known as La Calle Doce on the east side of town. Although larger in size than the town of Fillmore, Santa Paula also held obstacles for Mexican Americans: segregated schools, segregated movie theaters, and separate churches. Most of the Mexican population had limited job opportunities. The Merchants played against teams in Piru, Fillmore, and Oxnard. These two Santa Paula Merchants ballplayers in the photograph at left pose for an informal portrait after a game.

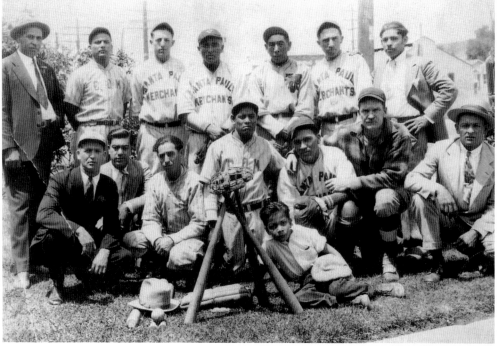

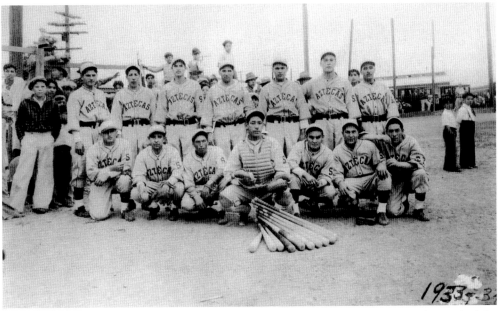

In 1933, the Santa Paula Aztecas were one of two teams made up of players who worked for Teague-McKevett in Santa Paula. The association camp was located along Santa Paula Creek on the eastern side of town in the barrio.

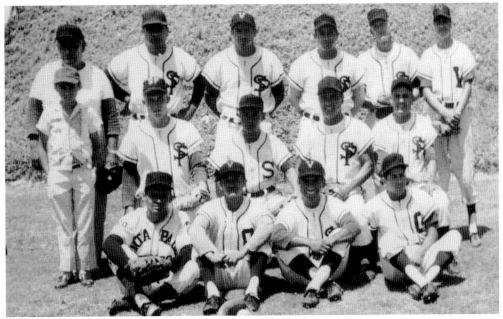

The 1961 Ventura County Merchants baseball team was based in Santa Paula. Pictured here are, from left to right, (first row) ? Tipton, Ernie Alamillo, Eddie Carlos, and John Ramírez; (second row) batboy Bob Flores Jr., Jim Colborn, Ray Duran, Tony Vásquez, and Sam Márquez; (third row) manager Tony Rivera, Albert Mendoza, Bob Flores, Ben Osuna, Phil Woods, and Ray Flores. (Courtesy of Jeff Maulhardt.)

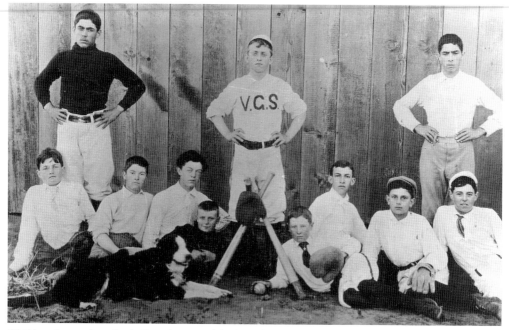

Children learned to play ball in their neighborhood streets and on school playgrounds. Ventura had its beginnings on the west side of the city, near the Mission San Buenaventura and the Ventura River. Ventura Grammar School was one of the first schools in Ventura. This 1895 photograph shows the school baseball team and its mascot. Among the boys are pitcher Fred Sánchez (first row, seventh from left) and Adam Rodríguez (second row, far left). (Courtesy of Museum of Ventura County.)

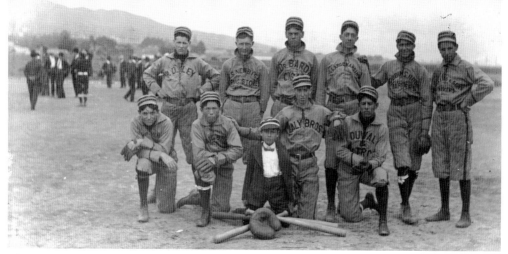

This 1902 Ventura city baseball team was unusual in that its players were sponsored by different businesses. The team's official name was the Ventura Juniors. The merchant names on the jerseys, familiar even today to local residents, include Bard, Duvall, and Lagomarsino. Among the players was a young man of Mexican descent named Charley Hall (second row, second from right), whose given name was Carlos Luís Hall. (Courtesy of Museum of Ventura County.)

Carlos Luís "Charley" Hall, a Mexican American born in Ventura in 1884 and raised there, played for the Ventura Juniors. He broke into baseball in 1904 as a pitcher with Seattle in the Pacific Coast League. He was sold to the Cincinnati Reds in 1906, and then went to Columbus and St. Paul until 1909, when he was traded to the Boston Red Sox and pitched through 1913. He compiled a 15-8 record with an ERA of 3.02 for the 1912 World Series champions. This was Fenway Park's inaugural season. (Courtesy of Museum of Ventura County.)

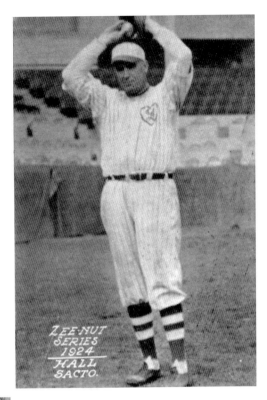

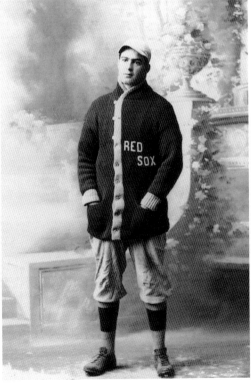

Charley Hall won the first game ever played at Fenway Park. In 1915, Hall set the American Association record for most consecutive wins at 16—the record was never broken. His career highlight was a game against the Detroit Tigers, when he struck out Ty Cobb, Sam Crawford, and Jim Delahanty in succession, known as Detroit's famed "Murderer's Row." Hall retired in 1925 and returned to Ventura, taking a job in law enforcement. He passed away in 1943 at the age of 59. (Courtesy of Museum of Ventura County.)

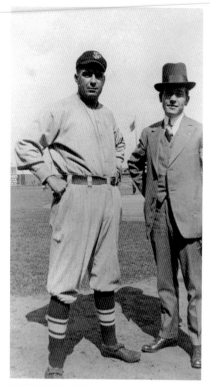

Charley Hall (left), called the "Sea Lion" because his deep voice echoed throughout the ballpark, hated another nickname, "The Greaser." Those were fighting words, and Charley got into plenty of fights. However, in 1922, while playing for St. Paul, Hall's catcher was a Cuban player, Mike González. Bunny Brief, the American Association's home-run leader at the time, came to the plate. Hall and González began to jabber in Spanish, and Brief became so unnerved that he struck out. (Courtesy of Museum of Ventura County.)

Golden State was a milk bottler with dairies and creameries in Ventura and Oxnard. It handled a third of the milk sold in California, and its fleet of delivery trucks was the largest in the state. Masón Covarrubias (first row, third from left) played for the Golden State Dairy 1930 Oxnard team. Covarrubias's father owned a saddle and harness shop and a large house with a yard. His son Chuck Covarrubias remembers that hundreds of townspeople attended his father's barbecues. (Courtesy of Museum of Ventura County.)

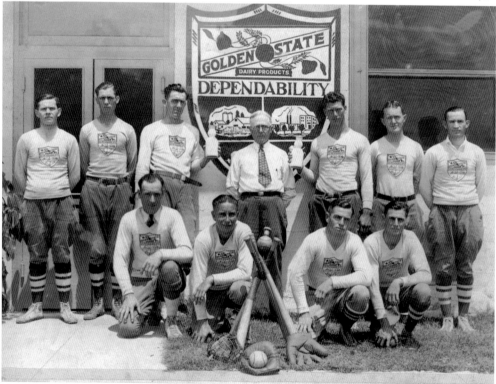

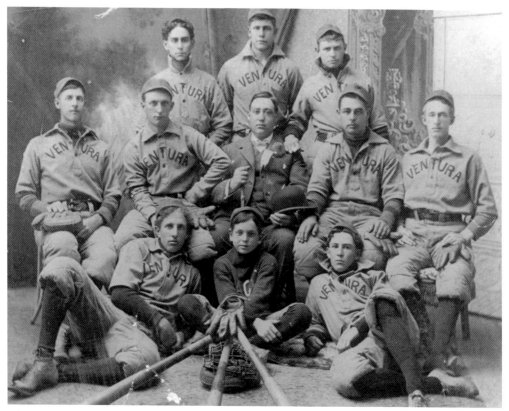

The 1902 Ventura Baseball Club included a popular ball player by the name of Mando Rivera. Pictured from left to right are (front row) Myron Gabbert, Ed Hearne, and Bert Browne; (second row) George Johnson, J. Mitchell, John Spear, Charlie Kaiser, and Walter E. Johnson; (third row) Mando Rivera, John Barnett, and George Dixon.

The 1930s Ventura All-Star Team was sponsored by Zanders clothing store. George Zander, a Jewish immigrant who had fled Nazi Germany in 1938 with his family, came to Ventura, where he opened a clothing business. Posing here are, from left to right, (first row) Marty Flores, Sal González, and Bill Flores; (second row) ? Peters, Phil Marquez, Joe Lorenzana, and Jack Wigton; (third row) Art Lillie, Chuck McIntire, Ellsworth Suytar, and Cephas González. (Courtesy of Museum of Ventura County.)

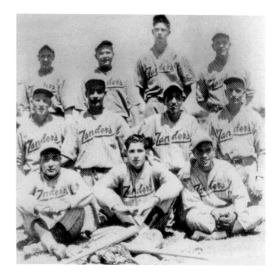

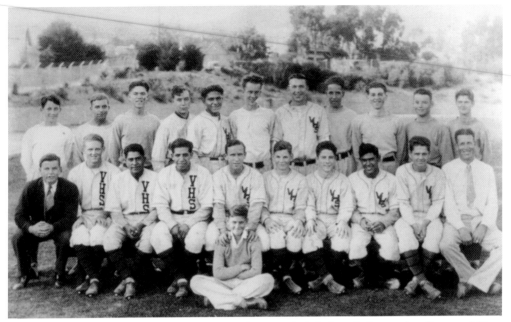

The 1930 Ventura High School team, shown here, included, from left to right, (first row) Don Burum, Bill Dysart, Herminio Cobos, Juan García, Clyde Wooley, Don Lang, Ray Faulk, Bill Flores, Kenneth Nugent, and coach ? Kolberg; (second row) Albert Barnes, Jack Wigton, Harold Holub, Harlan Lamp, Juan Macias, Norman Morrison, Walter Poplin, Bill Chaffee, Harold Kingston, Bob Sorem, and Wesley Fraser; the batboy is unidentified. Some of the players were from the Tortilla Flats barrio. (Courtesy of Museum of Ventura County.)

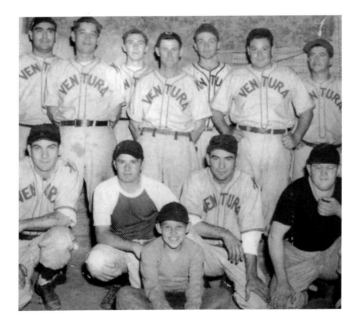

The Ventura Knights of Columbus hall was located downtown on Figueroa Street near the Mission San Buenaventura. The Knights sponsored ball teams. This is the 1948 Ventura K of C softball team. From left to right are, (first row) Dick Lang, Johnny Moss, batboy Butch Griego, Jack Lang, and Don Sloniker; (second row) Phil Marquez, Ed Griego, Gene Brooks, Bob Henry, Dalt Clements, Marian Amescua, and Ted Venegas. (Courtesy of Jeff Maulhardt.)

Tony Frank Moraga (right) and his friend Victor Castro pose for a photograph in 1900. They played baseball for Montalvo, an unincorporated area of Ventura. Moraga, a pitcher on the team, was the son of Octaviano and Rosario Moraga, who arrived from Sonora, Mexico, in the 1870s. He worked with his father, running the stagecoach line between Montalvo and Port Hueneme. Tony Moraga invented the portable horse-clipping machine. Until he died, he never missed a ball game in the vicinity. (Courtesy of Frank Moraga.)

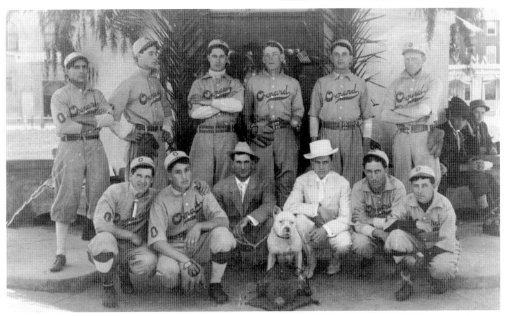

Oxnard began its life as an agricultural community, but by 1897 a new city had emerged when the Oxnard brothers introduced the sugar beet industry. Mexicans lived in La Colonia, the city barrio, located on the east side. In the middle of the city was Plaza Park, which had a gazebo in the center. In this 1915 photograph, an Oxnard team poses in front of that pagoda. Harry Tico (first row, second from right) is the uncle of Chuck Covarrubias of Oxnard. (Courtesy of Chuck Covarrubias.)

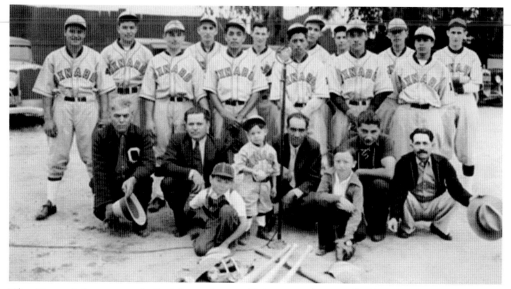

The Oxnard Aces was a ball club made up of Mexican players who brought notoriety to the community. As with other well-known local teams, they competed against Ventura County teams and those from Southern California, including African American semipro teams. John Ponce Lara (third row, second from right), grandfather of Antonio Magana, played for the Aces. A good third baseman, John was the son of migrant workers who traveled up the coast to Santa Maria during the picking season. (Courtesy of Antonio Magana.)

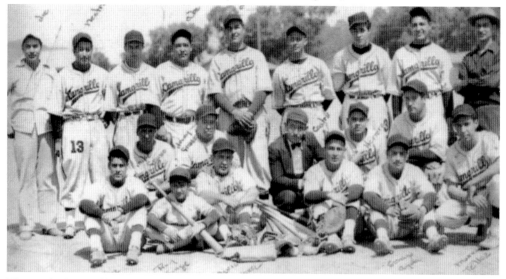

The 1950 Camarillo Merchants were a mix of two teams: the Blue Sox and the Merchants. Shown here are, from left to right, (first row) Chapo Hernández, Ron Singh, David Velásquez, unidentified, Genaro Ayala, and Manuel Téllez; (second row) Mike Franco, Johnny Franco, umpire ? Castro, ? Herrera, unidentified; (third row) Joe Velásquez, Néstor Álvarez, unidentified, Abe Franco, Jess Sánchez, George Bell, Manuel Ortiz, Louie López, and Demetrio Ayala. (Courtesy of Jeff Maulhardt.)

GREATER CENTRAL COAST

The greater Central Coast stretches as far north as the majestic Hearst Castle in San Simeon, to the California missions of San Luis Obispo, Lompoc, Solvang, and Santa Barbara, the scenic seaside towns of Cayucos, Morro Bay, Avila, and Pismo Beach to Santa Barbara. Also included are the rich farmlands of Arroyo Grande, Nipomo, Santa Maria, Guadalupe, Lompoc, and Los Alamos. Many ethnic groups settled in this region, including the Swiss, Swiss Italians, Portuguese, Japanese, Filipinos, and Mexicans. Mexican families date back prior to statehood, while other Mexicans came mainly from New Mexico, Texas, Colorado, and Mexico. A social consequence of this ethnic diversity has been mixed marriages and new subcultures throughout the Central Coast.

The economy was diverse, with farmlands, cattle, dairies, sugar plants, construction, packinghouses, and railroads. Mexicans and Filipinos worked in the fields. After school, on weekends, and holidays, it was common to see girls working in the fields and boys cutting and loading produce; there was no time for play. But, with the modernization of field machinery, sons and daughters had time to participate in sports, especially after World War II. Sundays became a day of barbecues and playing baseball and softball. Farming leagues were formed within produce companies as friendly competition as well.

The Bracero Program in the late 1940s and 1950s helped supplement the workforce, thus giving young people more time to become involved in community and school sports since they did not have to work in the fields after school. Baseball was popular among braceros who had played ball in their hometowns. Baseball and other sports have played major roles in allowing young people to stay in school, go to college on scholarships, and secure professional careers. Many professionals have returned to their communities, becoming community and political leaders, teachers and administrators, coaches, and business representatives.

The Central Coast has produced outstanding players and teams since 1902. Today, thousands of young people and adults play baseball and softball throughout the Central Coast, a fitting tribute to the early trailblazers.

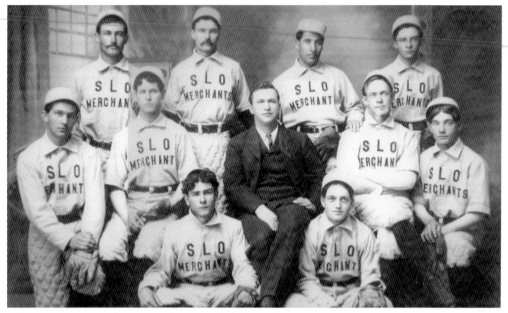

The 1902 San Luis Obispo Merchants included Frank Villa (third row, second from right). Frank, born in 1885, was a seventh-generation Californian residing in Cayucos. He played ball as a young man. In 1912, he and his partner started the Coast Truck and Garage Company, bringing the dairymen's milk to the creamery in San Luis Obispo each day. In 1922, he purchased a farm in San Miguel. The family-owned auto-repair facility remains the largest in the county. (Courtesy of John Villa.)

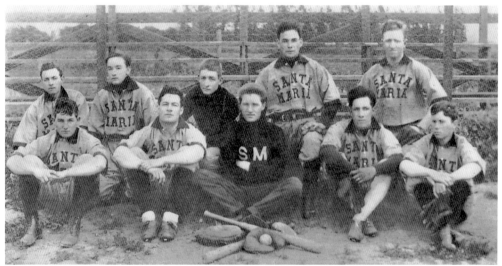

Claude Aguirre (first row, second from right), born in 1895, played at Santa Maria High School in 1913 and 1914, one of the first Mexican Americans to play sports at the school. He served in Siberia with the American Expeditionary Force in 1918 and was discharged in 1920. He coached and played with the Garey Tigers. He had seven children. His five sons served in the military: two in World War II and three in the Korean War. (Courtesy of Vernon Aguirre.)

GREATER CENTRAL COAST

The 1933 Santa Maria High School team was the California Interscholastic Federation (CIF) champions. Ray Aguirre (left side, first from bottom) came from a family of players. His father, Claude, was a ball player, and his brother Marcus played in the late 1920s. The team mirrored the rich diversity of Santa Maria, when agriculture employed Mexicans, Japanese, Portuguese, and Filipinos. Also pictured is Les Weber (left, second from top), who once brushed back Stan Musial, causing a major brawl between the Dodgers and Cardinals. (Courtesy of Santa Maria High School.)

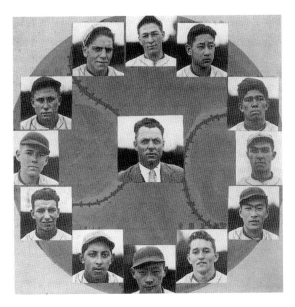

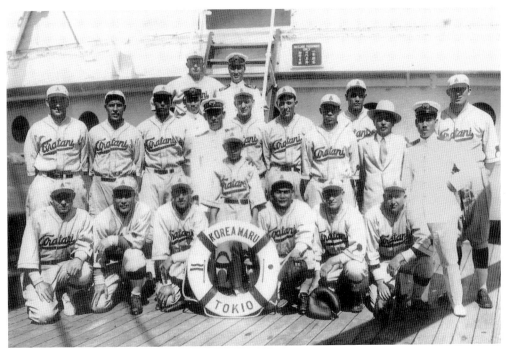

Baseball enthusiast Setsuo Aratani (second row, second from right in suit) sponsored a team from Guadalupe and Santa Maria that traveled to Japan in 1928. The team is shown onboard a boat in San Francisco. Two Mexican American brothers, Frank (second row, second from left) and Tony Montez (second row, third from left) helped win 27 out of 30 games. The boy in the center is George Aratani, the son of Setsuo, who was the founder of Mikasa Tableware and cofounder of Kenwood Electronics. (Courtesy of Tetsuo Furukawa.)

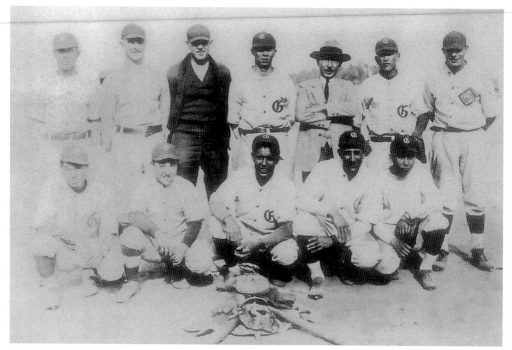

Guadalupe Produce, owned by Setsuo Aratani, hired workers who were also baseball athletes. Frank Montez (first row, center) and his brother Tony (not shown) had traveled to Japan in 1928 as members of the Aratani baseball team. Frank was very active in Guadalupe as a youth baseball coach, umpire, and Boy Scout leader. In addition, he served Guadalupe as a fireman in 1940 and was known as an outstanding automobile mechanic. (Courtesy of Toru Miyoshi.)

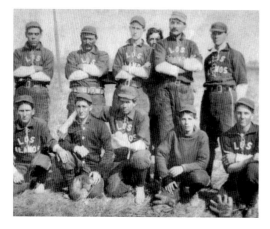

This early 1930s Los Alamos team included Mexican Americans. Bob Duboux (second row, far left) was born to a French father and Mexican mother. He graduated from Santa Maria High School in 1932. He later became a teamster, driving teams of six to eight horses for the Doheny Ranch, hauling grains from ranches to the warehouse. Pete Martínez (second row, second from right) was an outstanding hitter. He worked as a cook for the Holt Guest Ranch in Los Alamos. (Courtesy of John Rodríguez.)

GREATER CENTRAL COAST

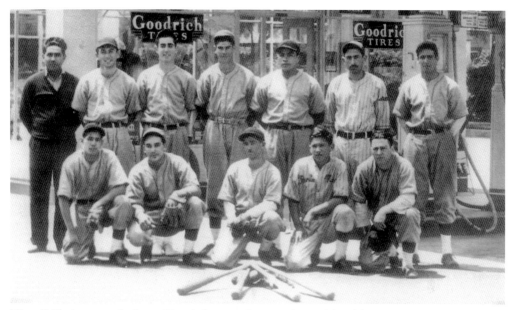

This 1937 photograph shows Terry's Service Station. Several local businesses in Santa Barbara County sponsored baseball teams. Posing here are, from left to right, (first row) Frank Brumana, George Leguas, Pete Brumana, Marshall Brumana, and Butch Simas; (second row) Romaldo Calderón (manager), Art Pimental, Arthur Silva, Lloyd DeRosa, Marcelino Almaguer, Onnie Herman, and Al Pimental. Like many teams of this era, the players represented the ethnic diversity of the larger community. (Courtesy of Smokey Silva.)

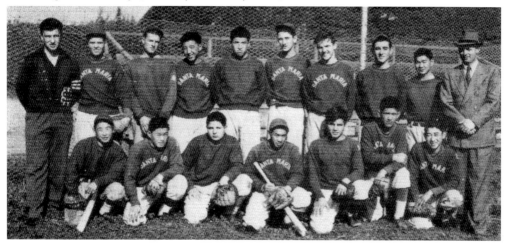

This ethnically mixed 1939 varsity team at Santa Maria High School includes John Ríos (second row, fifth from left), who later worked in the oil fields for the Union Oil Company. Arthur Silva (second row, eighth from left) played minor-league baseball before enlisting in the Army Air Force three days before the bombing of Pearl Harbor. He served four years as a gunner on B-24 and B-17 airplanes, flying 34 missions. Abe Trujillo (first row, third from left) served in World War II in the South Pacific with the navy; he later worked in oil field construction. (Courtesy of Santa Maria High School.)

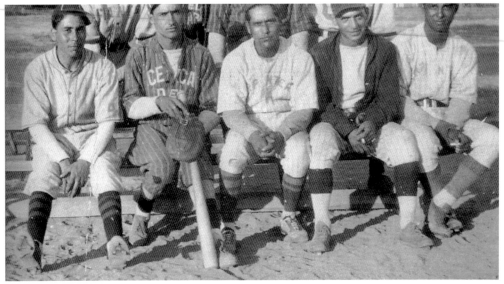

The Cerca del Mar baseball team was organized for a short period of time in the early 1930s. Like the Carpinteria Merchants team of this period, the players were an ethnically integrated mix of the best athletes in the Valley. Shown here are, from left to right, Albert Sánchez, Joe Goena, Sabino García, Joe Pérez, and an unidentified player. (Courtesy of Ernie Sánchez.)

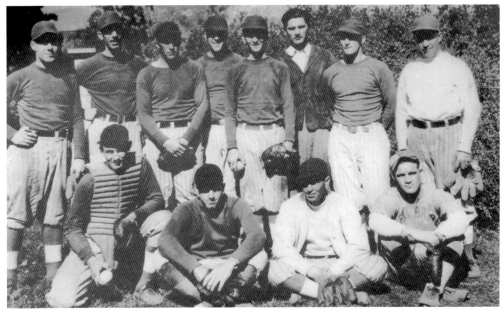

More than 50 Mexican Americans from Carpinteria served during World War II. When Mexican American veterans returned home, they confronted discrimination and prejudice once again. Fighting for their civil rights, they formed baseball teams as a political strategy to unite the community. Nationwide, Mexican American groups filed lawsuits against educational discrimination. The Montoya case in Carpinteria prompted an attorney to give his legal opinion that the city's segregation was illegal. The school board voted to end segregated schools.

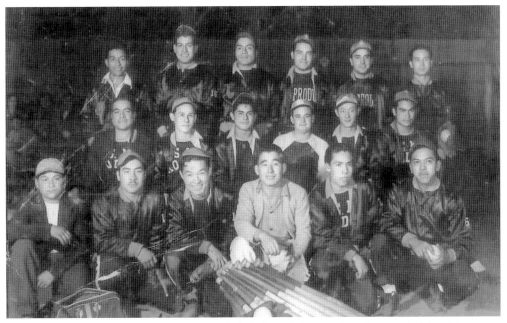

The 1941 Santa Maria Produce team included, from left to right, (first row) Félix Almaguer, Carmel Almaguer, two unidentified, Joe Ramírez, and Toby Hernández; (second row) Chicho Almaguer, unidentified, Lawrence Almaguer, two unidentified, and Jesús Almaguer; (third row) Tony Almaguer, Lindy Almaguer, Lucky Almaguer, Jackie Escalante, and two unidentified. Tony Almaguer coached youth sports, and Lindy Almaguer received the Purple Heart during World War II. (Courtesy of Guadalupe Cultural Arts and Educational Center/Sports Hall of Fame.)

This 1941 Rojas team included two Mexican American players: Frances Rojas (first row, center) and Vincent González (third row, far right). Rojas also coached the women's team, the Guadalupe Rock-Etts; moreover, he was involved with youth sports as chief umpire and volunteer. (Courtesy of Guadalupe Cultural Arts and Educational Center/ Sports Hall of Fame.)

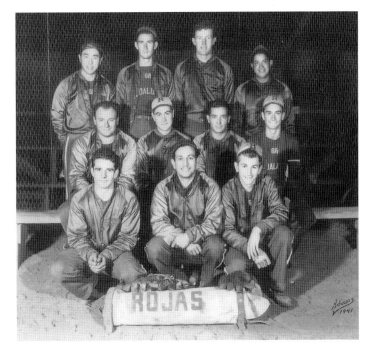

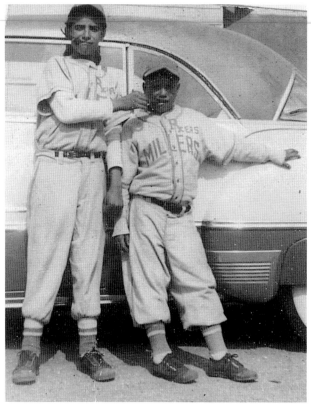

Brothers Joe (left) and Paul Bendele are seen in Lompoc, California, in 1952; at the time, Joe was 12 years old and Paul was 10. Both boys were natives of Texas but moved to Santa Maria at an early age. Paul pitched a perfect game in Middle League, striking out 21 of 21 batters in seven innings. He later pitched for the semiprofessional Santa Maria Indians in the 1960s. He was a pitching ace. (Courtesy of Paul Bendele.)

Jesse Rodríguez was born in Bena, near Bakersfield, California. His family moved to San Luis Obispo, where he played high school football, basketball, and baseball. He graduated in 1941, serving in World War II with the 88th Infantry of the Fifth Army for Gen. George Patton. In 1945, he returned and played for the San Luis Obispo Junior College Vikings. He played for the semipro SLO Merchants (later the Blues) at Mission Field. Rodríguez coached his son's Little League team. (Courtesy of John Rodríguez.)

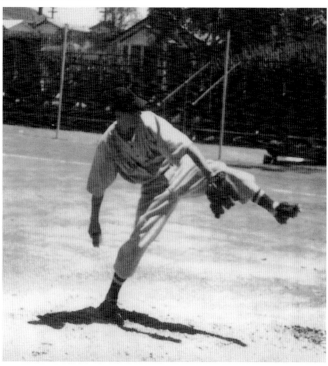

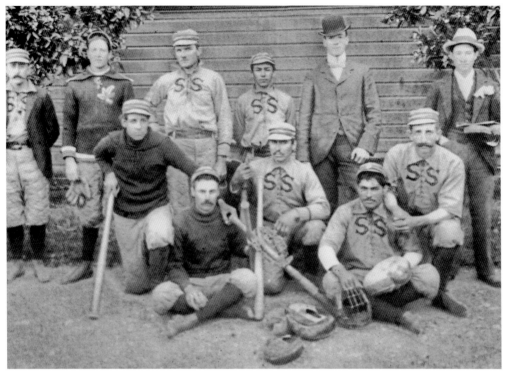

The 1900s Sycamore Springs team played in the Avila area, near Hot Springs. Among the players shown here are Alex Goodchild (third row, fourth from left) and his brother Richard (second row, center). Their maternal grandparents, Eduarda del Carmen Ocuna and William Benjamin Foxen, were pioneers of the Sisquoc Valley. Native Americans gave William the title "Don Julián" during the Mexican American War of 1846. He led John C. Fremont through his property to take Santa Barbara, which eventually led to the conquest of California. (Courtesy of John Rodríguez.)

Harry Goodchild is seen batting in 1949. He helped start Little League in Santa Maria and was one of its first coaches. His grandmother was Maria Antonia Ontiveros, a descendent of Juan Pacifico Ontiveros, a 17th-century pioneer of the Santa Maria Valley. In the stands are cousins Leo Julian and Sylvestre Pili. They married Isabel and Antonia DeLeon, respectively, from Texas. They were parents to Ariston Julian and Rennie Pili, who were standouts in youth baseball, high school, and college. (Courtesy of Harry Goodchild.)

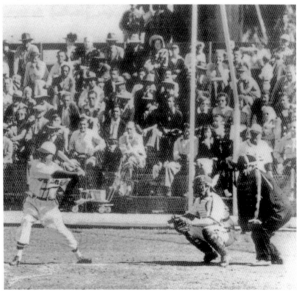

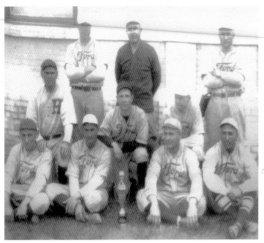

This photograph is of the 1923 Ford team, which won the Santa Barbara County championship. Benjamin H. Romero (first row, far right) was born and raised in Santa Barbara. While playing baseball, he met his wife in San Luis Obispo. He worked for Owen T. Rice in Santa Maria and Tani-Tab Farms in Oso Flaco. He is the father of Rock-Etts player Dorothy Romero Oliveira. (Courtesy of Dorothy Romero Oliveira.)

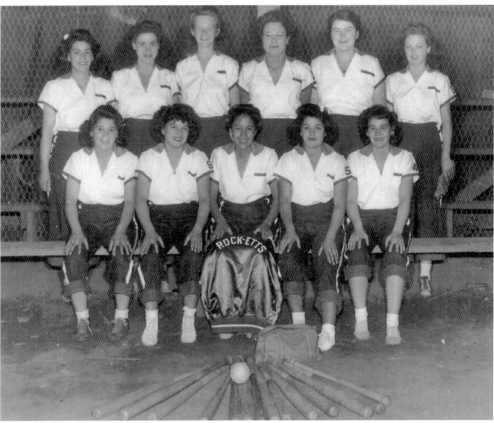

Benjamin H. Romero had a daughter, Dorothy, who was an outstanding player. She (first row, center) played for the Guadalupe girls' softball team, the Rock-Etts, seen here in 1945. The team was ethnically diverse, with most of the girls being of Portuguese and Swiss decent. Bernice Holmes (second row, fourth from left) and Etta Lee Holmes (second row, far right) were mother and daughter. Most of the women worked in the packing sheds, sorting and tying broccoli, cabbage, and lettuce. (Courtesy of Art Amarillas.)

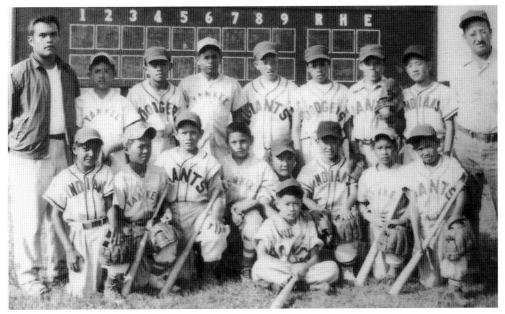

The 1957 Guadalupe All-Star team was coached by Fred Lizalde (second row, far left). Robert Sánchez (second row, third from right) was in the Army and retired as a deputy sheriff. Alfred Ramos (first row, third from left) served with Special Forces. Tommy Lara (second row, second from left) served in Vietnam. Rubén Arce (first row, far left) served in Korea. Lenny Lizalde (first row, fourth from left) is Fred's brother. (Courtesy of Guadalupe Cultural Arts and Education Center/Sports Hall of Fame.)

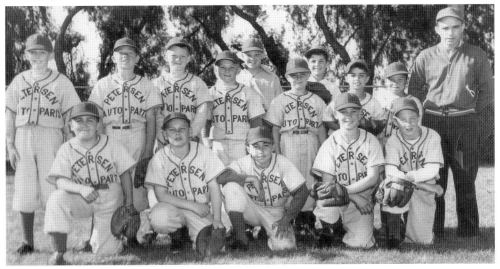

This 1950 Santa Maria team was sponsored by Peterson Auto Parts. Peter Paul Lucero (second row, second from right) was born in Colorado in 1941. He was on the first Little League baseball team to reach the regional finals. He lettered in three sports: football, baseball, and basketball. After serving in the military, he taught for 30 years in the Lucia Mar School District. Also included in this photograph is Gilbert Higuera (front row, third from left). (Courtesy of Ernie Corral.)

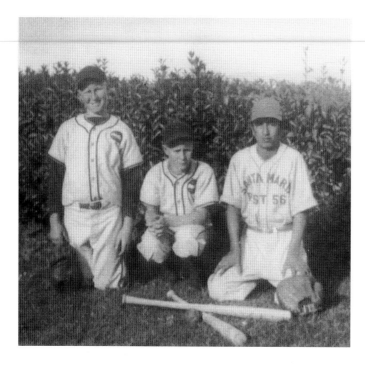

Rudy Galván (right) was born in East Los Angeles in 1934. His family moved to Santa Maria, where his father was a field worker. Rudy graduated from Santa Maria High School, where he was a member of Club Chicano. He and his three brothers joined the 82nd Airborne Division. Rudy served in Japan and Korea during the cold war and then worked for 39 years in management with the *Santa Maria Times*. He played 24 years of semipro ball. (Courtesy of Rudy Galván.)

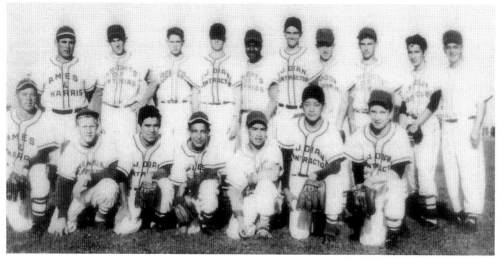

There are at least four Mexican Americans on this 1952 Middle League All-Stars of Santa Maria team: Bill Lozano, James Robles, Ernie Corral, and Frank Martínez. Their coach was Jim Cobb, the son of Ty Cobb. Lozano served in the military with two tours in Vietnam and retired as a full colonel. He spent 20 years in Germany and three years at the Pentagon. After the service, Bill was a manager in the aerospace industry, building military aircraft. Later, he became health care administrator for Medical Groups and Surgery Centers. (Courtesy of Ernie Corral.)

Rudy Salvador Martínez, born in Lompoc in 1936, played baseball, football, and basketball for the Lompoc Braves. He enrolled at the University of Southern California and later joined the Marines. He pitched the first game in the 1956 Olympics for the United States, the first time that baseball had been seen at the Olympics; the United States won 11-5. Later, Rudy toured the Pacific, pitching in the Marine Division and being voted the outstanding tournament player when he pitched a no-hitter. (Courtesy of Bobby Martínez.)

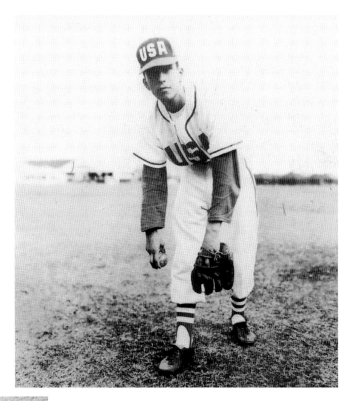

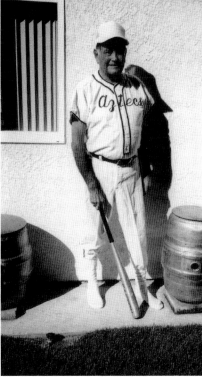

Art Gallego Amarillas was born in Santa Maria in 1939. He played in 1952 with the Little League Indians and with the Middle League while playing night softball. In 1958, he was stationed in Guam with the Navy. He played against the 1959 US All-Stars in Japan and had drinks with Whitey Ford. Amarillas played and managed ball in 1962 with the Santa Maria Aztecas. He was elected president of the South Side Little League for six years. (Courtesy of Art Amarillas.)

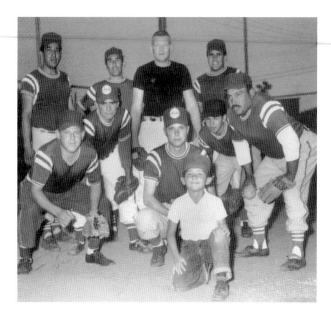

The 1960 Avis softball team included, from left to right, (first row) unidentified, Joe Bendele, Armando Bargas, and Vincent Galván; (second row) Armando Torres, Benny Hidalgo, unidentified, and Mickey Pardo; the batboy is Armando Torres Jr. Joe was an all-star infielder, and he and his brother Paul (not shown) played baseball and softball. Joe's son, Joe Jr., was also a baseball player, earning All-CIF (California Interscholastic Federation) second-team honors. (Courtesy of Joe Bendele.)

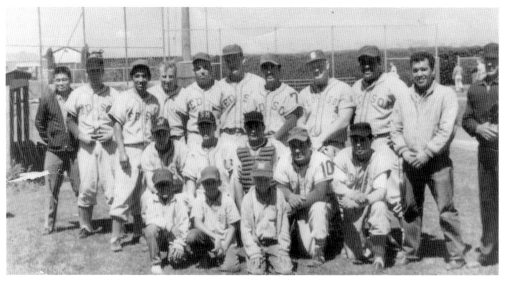

The 1960 Guadalupe Red Sox included Blas Torres (second row, second from right), who served during the Korean War. He played military softball and boxed in the Eighth Army Tournament, winning the lightweight championship. After his military career, he was a roofer, retiring after 38 years. Rudy Galván (third row, seventh from left) remains active in a military color guard unit known as "Boots and Chutes." Also pictured are coach Louis Olivo (third row, third from right) and manager Jerry Navarro (third row, second from right). (Courtesy of James Bartlett.)

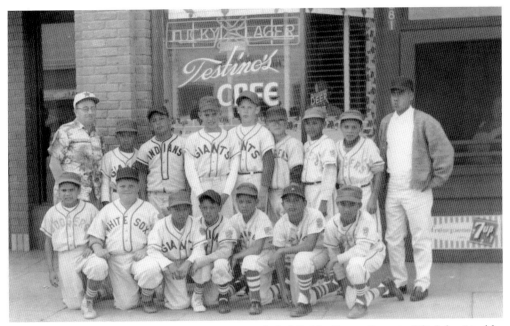

The 1961 Guadalupe Little League All-Stars included Bobby Rivas, Rennie Pili, John Lizalde, Richard Noriega, and Manny Hernández. Rennie (first row, third from right) played in the Guadalupe Pee Wee League, making several all-star teams. He attended Hancock Junior College, making all-league and all-conference in 1968 and 1969. At California State–Los Angeles, he made all-league second team. Rennie played three years for the Santa Maria Indians. He served on the Guadalupe City Council and served as mayor. (Courtesy of Rennie Pili.)

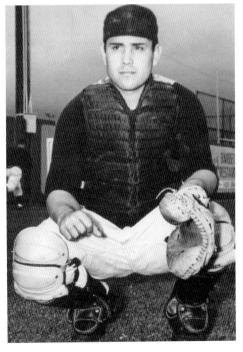

Milo Lizalde is about to warm up pitcher George Vásquez in 1962. Both Vásquez and Lizalde were signed by the Pittsburgh Pirates. Vásquez played with the likes of Roberto Clemente, Manny Sanguillén, and Willie Stargell. The Pirates sent Lizalde to play ball in Las Vegas with a semiprofessional team comprised largely of college students, many of who eventually made it to the major leagues. (Courtesy of John Lizalde.)

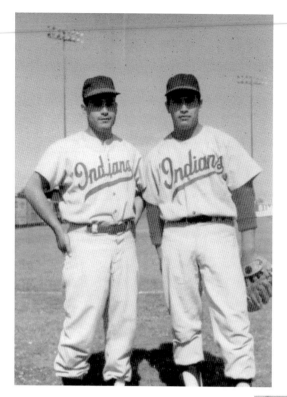

Brothers Milo (left) and John Lizalde loved playing baseball. Milo was drafted into the Army in 1966 and stationed at Fort Ord in Northern California. On the weekends, he would come home and play for the Santa Maria Indians semipro ball club. John, who was a junior in high school at the time, played with his brother that summer with the Indians. (Courtesy of John Lizalde.)

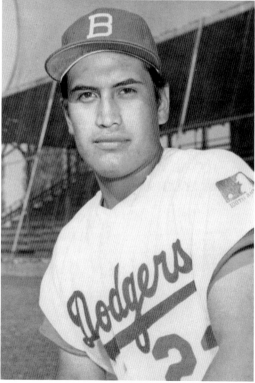

John Lizalde lettered in several sports at Righetti High School and lettered in football and baseball at Hancock Junior College, playing for legendary coaches Barney Eames and John Osborne. Lizalde was voted Most Valuable Player in 1969. He also played at Gonzaga University when the 1971 team advanced to the district finals of the NCAA Tournament. He later played third base in the Los Angeles Dodgers' minor-league system at Bakersfield under coach Ducky LeJohn. Lizalde taught at El Camino Junior High and served on the Guadalupe City Council. (Courtesy of John Lizalde.)

The 1965 Santa Maria Middle League team included John Jimenez (third row, third from left), later a teacher of Chicano history for 37 years. His brother Francisco (not shown) is a professor and author at Santa Clara University. Ralph Baldievez (second row, fourth from left) played youth ball and became the athletic director at Santa Maria High School, where the football stadium was named after him. Eddie Navarro (second row, far left) played Little League and varsity baseball at Santa Maria High School for three years. (Courtesy of Eddie Navarro.)

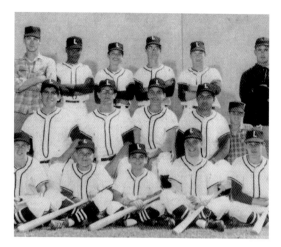

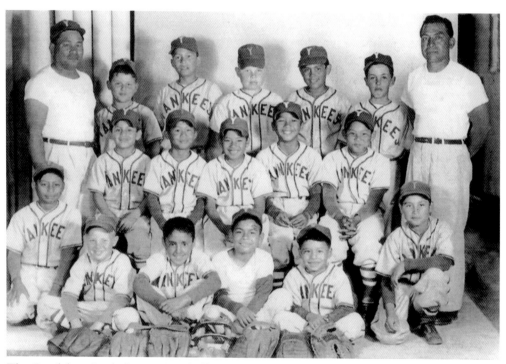

The Guadalupe Little League Baseball Yankees won the 1955 championship. Ariston Julian is in the first row, far right. Ariston's mother, Isabel DeLeon, was raised in Texas, and his father, Leo Julian, was of Filipino background. Ariston played four years of varsity high school baseball, two years of varsity football, and also wrestled in high school. He won awards in high school and community college and went on to play for the Santa Maria Indians as well as in the Air Force. (Courtesy of Guadalupe Cultural Arts and Education Center/Sports Hall of Fame.)

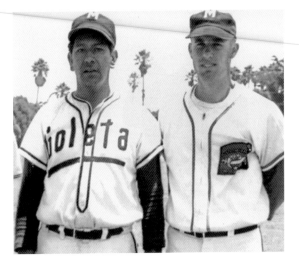

Ray Orosco (left), born in Austin, Texas, came to Santa Barbara and worked in construction, including at UCSB. He had a chance to play professional ball but opted to raise a family. His passion, however, continued, and he sponsored the Goleta Merchants and played for and managed the Santa Barbara Jets. Orosco maintained Laguna Park Stadium for games. His son Jesse played at Santa Barbara High School and later for several major-league teams. (Courtesy of the Ray Orosco family.)

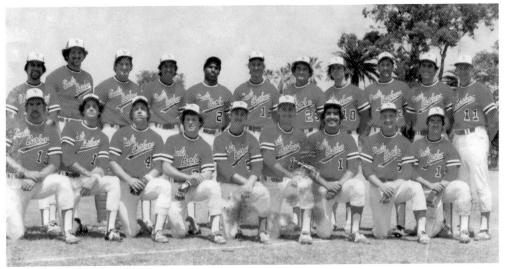

Jesse Orosco (second row, fourth from left), born in 1957 in Santa Barbara, played for Santa Barbara High School. In 1983, he won 13 games with the New York Mets, saved 17 games, made the all-star team, and finished third in the National League Cy Young Award voting. The following season, he had 31 saves. He was on the mound against the Boston Red Sox in 1986, striking out the last batter to give the Mets the world championship. (Courtesy of Jesse Orosco family.)

Jesse Orosco played for the Los Angeles Dodgers in 1988, winning his second World Series championship. He retired in 2003 at the age of 46, one of the oldest players in the modern age. Orosco is one of only 29 players in baseball history to have appeared in major-league games in four decades. He pitched in 1,252 games, which is the major-league record for appearances by a pitcher. (Courtesy of Jesse Orosco family.)

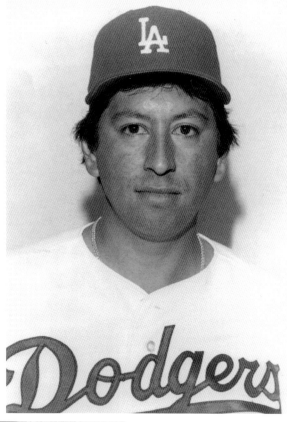

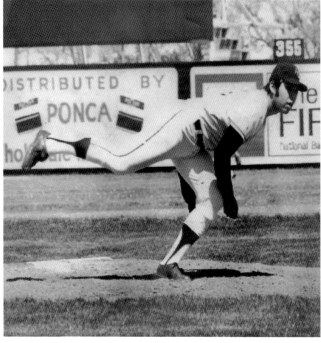

Frank Reyes was born in Camp Cook, California, in 1951 and played at Righetti High School and Hancock Junior College in Santa Maria. He signed with the Giants as a pitcher and was sent to their minor-league farm system. Reyes pitched for Great Falls in the Pioneer League, Fresno in the California League, and Amarillo in the Texas League, starting 49 minor-league games. After his baseball days, Reyes became a fireman, retiring after 32 years. (Courtesy of Guadalupe Cultural Arts and Education Center/Sports Hall of Fame.)

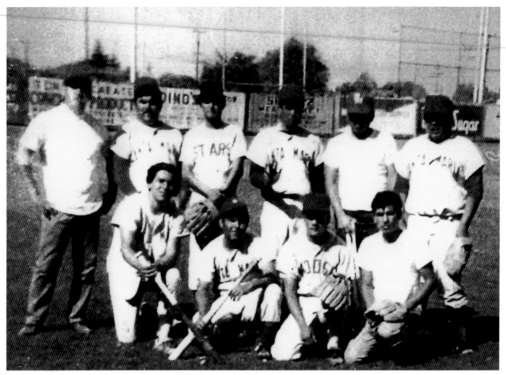

This 1970 team, Los Freseros, was comprised of strawberry workers. Pictured from left to right are (first row) Louie Marrufo, Polo Villareal, Sal Medina, and Jose Morin; (second row) Eddie Navarro, Bernie Morales, Manuel Villareal, Mike Lara, Mercedes Villareal, and Johnny Ríos. Lara was ambidextrous, pitching both left- and right-handed. Navarro was eventually promoted to foreman and later supervisor, where he still works with strawberry operations in Santa Maria. He, along with others, formed a Berry League with teams from other ranches, playing on Sundays. (Courtesy of Eddie Navarro.)

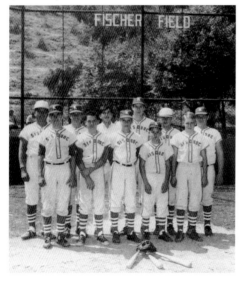

Sisquoc is southeast of Santa Maria. The 1965 team included Mike Brown (far left), whose mother is Chumash/Mexican; Gary Aguirre (fifth from left), whose mother, Vivian, played women's softball; Tim Penny (fourth from right), whose mother is from the Ontiveros family; John Rivas (third from right), who served in the Navy and worked in the oil fields; and Mike Nogues (second from right), who served in the Army. Nogues's grandmother's family (Chávez) worked the mines in the Santa Margarita area. (Courtesy of Vernon Aguirre.)

GREATER CENTRAL COAST

SACRAMENTO

Sacramento has always been recognized as a baseball town, and it has sent many ballplayers to the minor and major leagues. Baseball in Sacramento during the period from 1920 to 1960 was recognized as the only game in town. Games were played after Mass on Sundays, attended by spectators wearing their Sunday best. Many relationships were made at these games. The Mexican Athletic Club (MAC) of the 1930s, 1940s, and early 1950s was recognized as the dominant team in the Sacramento area.

The Mexican American Hall of Fame and Sports Association was established in 1973. It grew out of local Mexican American athletic leagues founded 80 to 90 years ago and because other halls of fame were not recognizing Latino athletes. The purpose of the hall of fame is twofold: to honor Mexican American athletes of the past and to assist youth in realizing their athletic potential.

One can be forgiven if the name Ernie Cervantes does not ring a bell, as his is hardly a household name. But, to Sacramento's Mexican American community, especially to its more seasoned sporting adherents, he is regarded as "Mr. Baseball." Cervantes was good enough to be offered a contract with the St. Louis Browns of the American League. He could run, hit, and was a pillar behind the plate. This was in the late 1930s, when few Mexican Americans made it to the big leagues. Understandably, Cervantes's seminal baseball exploits remain a wellspring of community pride.

Many factors over the last 50 years have changed the face of Mexican American baseball in Sacramento and Northern California: the phenomenal growth of cities and towns, the advent of television and televised major sports programs, the proliferation of independent and/or travelling athletic teams, restrictions on young Chicano athletes by high schools regarding outside sports activities, year-round obligations to train at high school facilities, and sociocultural pressures that detract from wholesome sports activities. The "good old days," when everybody knew each other and teams were more localized, no longer exist.

The best action for the Mexican American sports community is to exert more effort to foster, encourage, promote, advance, and create interest in the practice and enjoyment of sport activities among youth. Then, hopefully, the Mexican American community will be doing its best to maintain and enhance community pride.

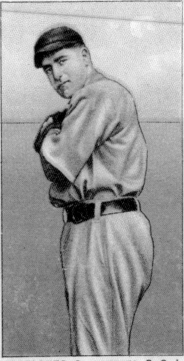

ARRELANES, SACRAMENTO, P. C. L.

Frank Arrellanes was born in Santa Cruz, California, in 1882. He played for the San Francisco Seals, San Jose Prune Pickers, Fresno Raisin Eaters, Santa Cruz Sand Crabs, Denver Bears, and Vernon Tigers. In 1908, Arrellanes became one of the first Latin players to play in the major leagues when he pitched for the Boston Red Sox; he posted a 24-22 win-loss record for the team. Arrellanes joined the Sacramento Senators near the end of the 1910 season and remained with the team through 1914. (Courtesy of Alan O'Connor.)

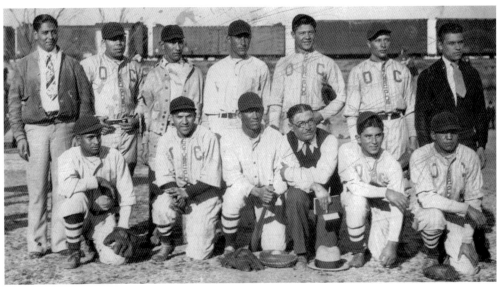

The 1920s Sacramento Mexican American Octubre Club was a forerunner of the Mexican Athletic Club (MAC), which formed in 1931. This photograph was taken at Twenty-first and C Streets. The ballpark (now Ulysses S. Grant Park) and Southern Pacific train tracks are visible in background. Outfielder Pete Benton is in the second row, second from left. In the second row, third from left, is Julio Resendez, an outstanding pitcher who once threw a 20-inning game. Resendez was a founder of the MAC. (Courtesy of Julius Resendez.)

SACRAMENTO

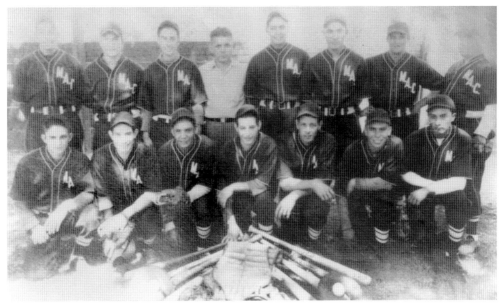

The Mexican Athletic Club (MAC) of Sacramento spanned from 1931 to 1957. Shown here in 1937 at the ballpark at Twenty-first and C Streets in Sacramento are, from left to right, (first row) Ernie Cervantes Sr., Jim Herrera, Ken Sánchez, Lupe Cisneros, Soco Trujillo, Chon Hernández, and Joe Hernández; (second row) Ted Sánchez, Eddie Trujillo, Ray Lujan, Pete Benton (manager), Jess Sánchez, Julian Cisneros, Abe Salgado, and Pete Urias. (Courtesy of Mexican American Hall of Fame Sports Association.)

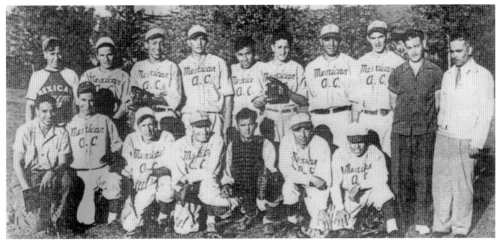

The 1930s MAC team beat the host San Francisco Mexican American team 9-4. The team also played Mexican American baseball teams in Merced, Stockton, Turlock, Tracy, Woodland, and the San Francisco Bay area. Shown here are, from left to right, (first row) unidentified, Corky Ramírez, unidentified, Jim Herrera, Ernie Cervantes Sr., Clifford Armendáriz, and Jessie González; (second row) Basilio Devila (manager), unidentified, Larry Gomes, Jess Sánchez, Tubby Ríos, Manual Márquez, Julian Cisneros, Bill Sarillana, Lupe Cisneros, and unidentified. (Courtesy of Mexican American Hall of Fame Sports Association.)

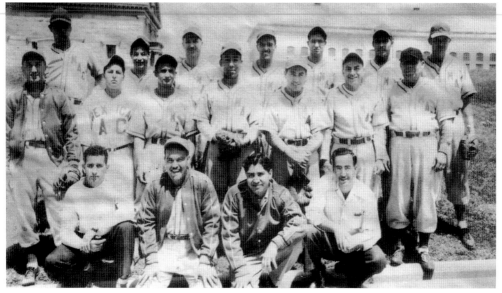

The Sacramento MAC team poses at Folsom Prison prior to playing an exhibition game in front of the prisoners or a game against the prisoners. Shown are, from left to right, (first row) unidentified Folsom Prison team manager, Frank Sánchez, Mose Cisneros, and Tony Guerra; (second row) John Stanich, Leo Cervantes, Ernie Cerventes Sr., Larry Gomes, Jess Torres, Richard Maldonado, and Pete Urias; (third row) unidentified, Lupe Cisneros, unidentified, Pete Benicio, Tony Alvarado, John Caranza, and Bill Sarillana. (Courtesy of Mexican American Hall of Fame Sports Association.)

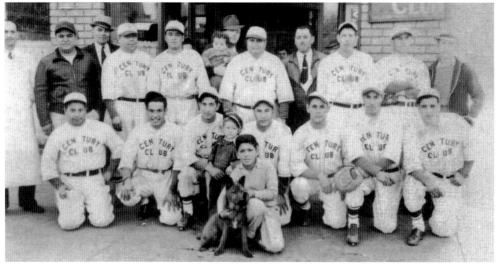

This is the Century Club ball team that won the pennant in the Federal Division of the Sacramento Winter Baseball League in 1939. Shown here are, from left to right, (first row) Ed Moreno, Frank Sánchez, Jack Trujillo, Richard Moreno (mascot), Ed Trujillo, Trini Campos, Jess Saucedo, and James Pérez; (second row) manager Joe García (in dark jacket and cap), Pete Urias, Charles García, Mario Moreno, Soco Trillo, John Cafarelli, and Julio Resendez (coach); Henry García is the batboy in the front. (Courtesy of Mexican American Hall of Fame Sports Association.)

American Legion baseball is amateur baseball that provides young men "an opportunity to develop their skills, personal fitness, leadership qualities, and to have fun." The program started in 1925 in South Dakota and, by the 1930s, had spread to the Sacramento Valley. Manhart Post No. 391 is a local team that has a very competitive history dating to the 1930s. Pictured here is Corky Ramírez playing Senior American Legion baseball (19 and under) in the late 1930s. (Courtesy of Tom Ramírez.)

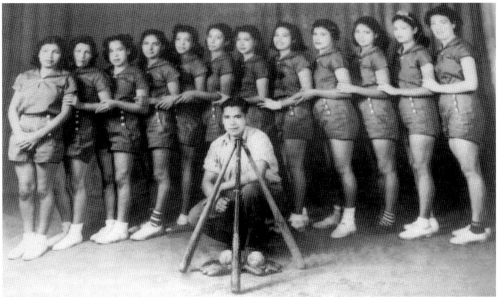

The 1930s Mexican Athletic Club softball team played in one of the city leagues in Sacramento. All of the young women were from the same neighborhood and represented the "cream of the crop." These players had exceptional skills, and the majority of the team played together for nearly four years. The team was coached by Basilio Dávila, who was later inducted into the Sacramento Mexican American Hall of Fame. (Courtesy of Mexican American Hall of Fame Sports Association.)

Ernie Cervantes Sr. was, at the age of 12, the only Mexican American playing on an all–African American team in San Antonio, Texas. The Sacramento Mexican American community regards Cervantes as "Mr. Baseball." He turned down a contract with the St. Louis Browns because he was married and making more money contracting trucks to the City of Sacramento. The Browns' offer took place in the 1930s, when Mexican Americans were unheard of in the major leagues. (Courtesy of Ernie Cervantes Jr.)

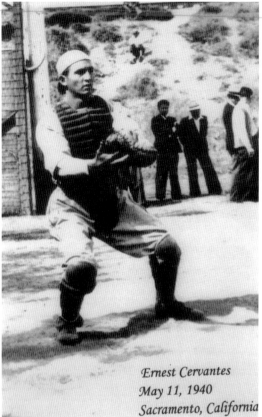

Ernest Cervantes
May 11, 1940
Sacramento, California

This 1940s Monks team finished second in the Girls' Division of the Sacramento City Municipal Night Softball League, which played at Roosevelt Park, at Tenth and P Streets. Josephine Barragán was one of the top players. Shown here are, from left to right, (first row) Mary Albrica, Teresa Rajas, Ann Stanich, Jean Bath, and Arleen Matson; (second row) Margaret Sousa, Hazel McKerros, Rosalie Hackett, Virginia Queirola, Josephine Barragán, Dolores Yenick, and Dorothy Rakestraw. Star pitcher Stanich was the first woman elected to the National Softball Hall of Fame. (Courtesy of Cuno Barragán.)

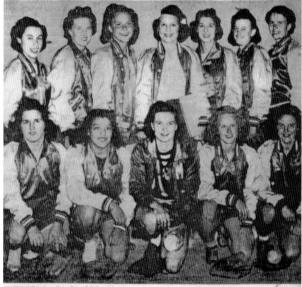

...ished Second in Race for Girls' Softball Crown

NNERUPS for the city girls' softball crown was this aggregation which performed under ...ner of Tom B. Monk. In front, left to right, are Mary Albricia, Teresa Rajas, Ann Stanich, ...h and Arleen Matson, while in back are Margaret Sousa, Hazel McKerros, Rosalie Hac Virginia Queirola, Josephine Barragan, Dolores Yenick and Dorothy Rakestraw.

Ernie Cervantes Jr. was the first and only batboy of the Sacramento Mexican Athletic Club; it was the start of a successful baseball career. Ernie went on to eventually play with the MAC "A" team as well as other local, county, college, and military service teams. This photograph was taken at the McKinley Park ball field in Sacramento. (Courtesy of Ernie Cervantes Jr.)

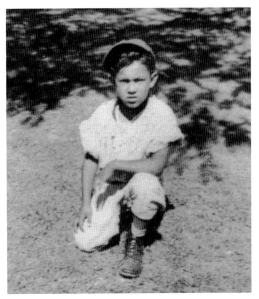

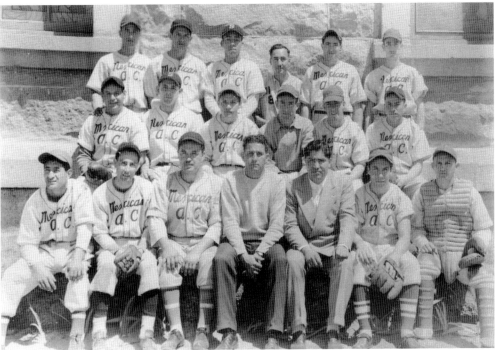

The Sacramento Mexican Athletic Club team sported new faces as men returned from World War II. The team poses in front of the chapel at Folsom Prison prior to an exhibition game. Shown here are, from left to right, (first row) Jackie Ramírez, Ray Lujan, Frank Sánchez, unidentified, Julian Cisneros, unidentified, and Ernie Cervantes Sr; (second row) Ted Sánchez, Trinidad Campos, three unidentified players, and Chon Hernández; (third row) Manual Cisneros, Bill Sarillana, Larry Gomes, Tony Guerra, Tony Alvarado, and unidentified. (Courtesy of Mexican American Hall of Fame Sports Association.)

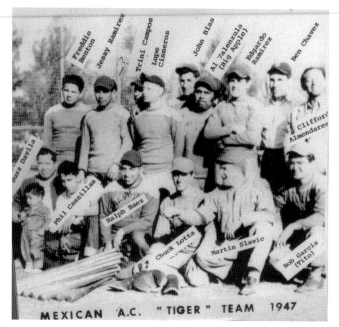

Freddie Benton · Jessy Ramirez · Trini Campos · Lupe Cisneros · John Blas · Al Zalenzula (Big Apple) · Edgardo Ramirez · Ben Chavez · Clifford Almendarez · Buzz Davila · Phil Cassillas · Ralph Baez · Chuck Lotta · Martin Slavic · Bob Garcia (Tito)

MEXICAN A.C. "TIGER" TEAM 1947

This is the post–World War II "Tiger" or "B" team of the Sacramento MAC. The names are clearly labeled on the photograph. Players like Chuck Lota, Lupe Cisneros, and Trini Campos were later promoted to the MAC "A" team. The 1947 image was taken at the ballpark at Twenty-first and C Streets in Sacramento. With returning war veterans and an economic upswing beginning, the MAC rosters swelled, as did all league rosters. (Courtesy of Mexican American Hall of Fame Sports Association.)

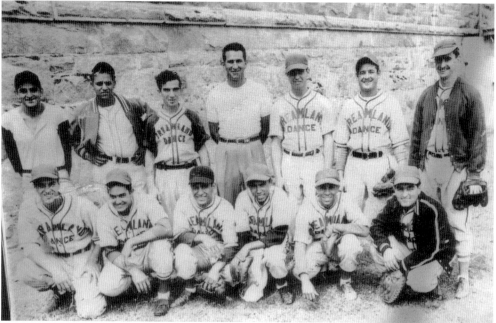

The Dreamland Dance sponsored a 1940s team comprised of Mexican Americans. The team is seen here in front of a wall of Folsom Prison prior to playing an exhibition game. Dreamland Dance was originally owned by Ed Kripp, a player in Sacramento in the 1890s and manager of the 1898 California League champion Sacramento Gilt Edge. Kripp owned and built the original professional baseball park at Riverside Boulevard and Broadway, called Buffalo Park, and later Edmonds Field in the 1940s and 1950s. (Courtesy of Mexican American Hall of Fame Sports Association.)

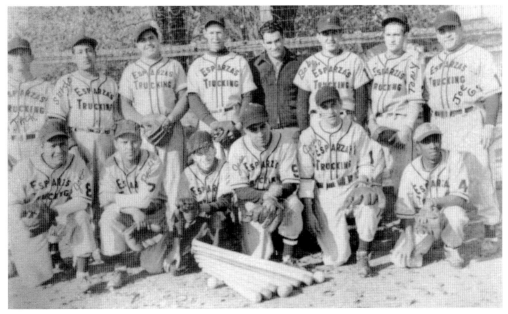

Esparza Trucking was a lower-division team in the Sacramento area that played on Sunday afternoons at local Sacramento ballparks. The team was sponsored by Jack Esparza (second row, center), owner of a trucking company. Esparza was no ballplayer, but he had a love of the game and stayed connected to the Mexican American community with his sponsorships. (Courtesy of Mexican American Hall of Fame Sports Association.)

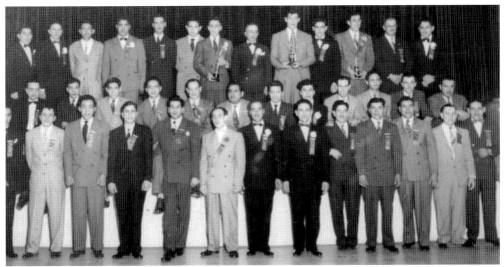

This 1947 photograph celebrates the 16th anniversary of the Club Atlético Mexicano. The Mexican Athletic Club was formed in 1931 to support a team, and it became a cultural force for Mexican Americans. In the 1930s and 1940s, MAC supported sports teams and social activities. MAC teams competed at the highest level of the Sacramento County and Winter Leagues. Local sportswriter Bill Conlin stated that MAC had a "splendid record for its charity work." (Courtesy of Mexican American Hall of Fame Sports Association.)

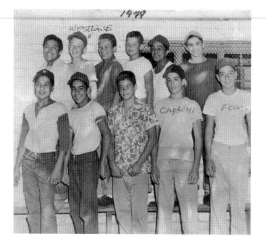

The 1949 California Upholstery baseball team won the championship of the Sacramento City Boys Summer League, 150 Pound Division. This 1949 photograph was taken at Sacramento's McKinley Park. Shown here are, from left to right, (first row) Louis Armendáriz, Ruben Placencia, Gil Laidlaw, Nick Capachi, and Ed Fowler; (second row) Everet Meléndez, Jim Westlake, Frank Eakes, Jim Feenstra, Alfonso Arroyo, and Manuel López. The old city leagues promoted baseball for Sacramento kids, including the Mexican American community. (Courtesy of Nick Capachi.)

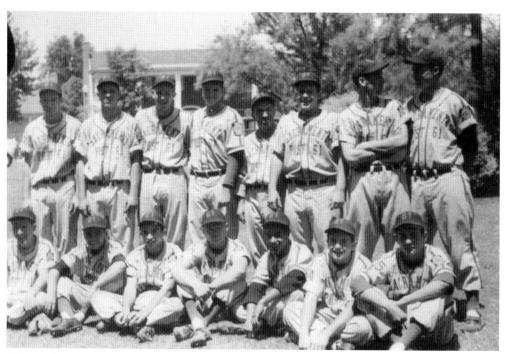

This is the 1951 Post No. 61 American Legion baseball team. Beginning immediately after World War II and through the 1970s, Post No. 61 was one of the top American Legion teams in California and featured the best talent in the area. The players are, from left to right, (first row) Bill Werry, Dick Alejo, Pete Stathos, Bob Ayers, Bob Gonsalves, Ray Lesdesma, and Bruce Parsons; (second row) Jim Fellos, Jan Aitken, Roger Herkowitz, Mike Toomey, George Lial, Don Deary, Dick Traversi, and Gene Hurych. (Courtesy of Jim Fellos.)

SACRAMENTO

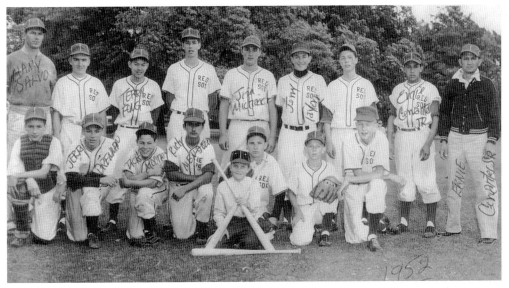

This 1952 photograph was taken at McKinley Park in Sacramento. The Red Sox were the winners of the Babe Ruth championship that year. Posing for the team photograph are, from left to right, (first row) unidentified, Jerry Brennan, Dick Mooney, Richard Mendoza, and three unidentified; (second row) Manny Salvo, unidentified, Terry Fong, unidentified, Jim Mickacich, Jerry Taylor, unidentified, Ernie Cervantes Jr., and Ernie Cervantes Sr. ("Mr. Baseball"); the batboy is unidentified. Salvo was a former major leaguer and Sacramento Solon. (Courtesy of Ernie Cervantes Jr.)

The Sacramento MAC team poses at Folsom Prison in the late 1940s. From left to right are (first row) Tony Alvarado, Mike Hernández, unidentified, Corky Ramírez, Ted Sánchez, and Paul Sánchez; (second row) Frank Ríos, Butch Granico, manager Manuel Ramírez, Pete Benicio, two unidentified, and former Sacramento Solon Curt Schmidt. The MAC team and the prison team, the Represa Eagles, played in the Sacramento County League. The Eagles were not, needless to say, a traveling team. (Courtesy of Gary Ríos.)

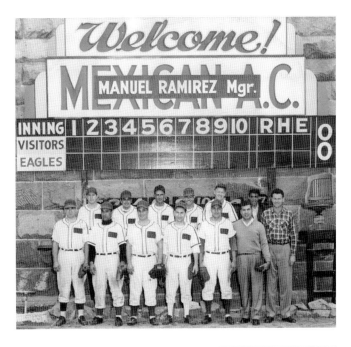

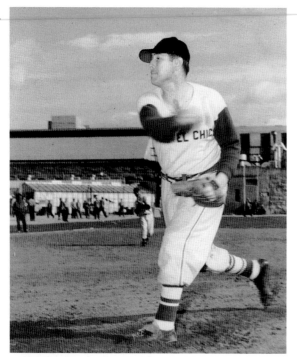

Frank Ríos warms up prior to a game at Folsom Prison. Ríos played for El Chico's restaurant in Sacramento, a block down the street from the home of the old Pacific Coast League Sacramento Solons. Frank played in the County League and Winter Leagues, often for the Mexican Athletic Club. El Chico and the prison team, the Represa Eagles, played in the Sacramento County League. Both of Frank's sons, Ed and Gary, went on to play professional baseball. (Courtesy of Gary Ríos.)

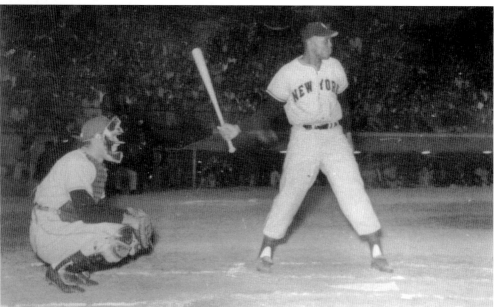

Cuno Barragán is seen here catching for Mexico's Central League All-Stars on October 1, 1957, before the start of Winter League. The team is playing the Willie Mays All-Stars in front of 30,000 fans in Mexico City. Mays is seen here at the plate. Mays's all-star team included major leaguers Bobby Avila, Gene Baker, Joe Black, Wes Covington, George Crowe, Elston Howard, Brooks Lawrence, Harry Simpson, and Al Smith. Barragán excelled defensively and went 2-3 at the plate. (Courtesy of Cuno Barragán.)

Cuno Barragán caught for the 1957 Puebla Pericos (Parrots) in the Winter League of the Mexico Central League. Early scouting reports indicated that he would be a "very effective catcher," however, a foul tip broke a finger on his throwing hand on opening day. His cousin in Sacramento, Dick Alejo, who caught for Sacramento Junior College, was called in to take Barragán's place behind the plate in October. Barragán is pictured here in the Pericos dugout with his finger bandaged. (Courtesy of Cuno Barragán.)

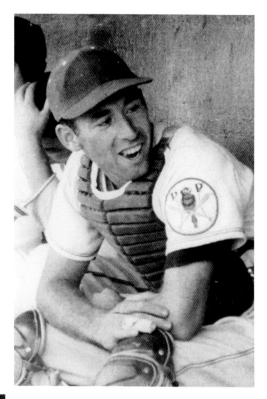

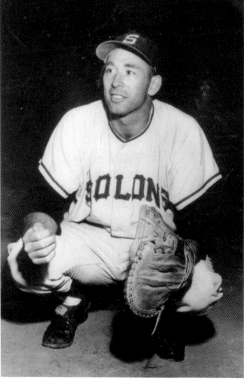

Cuno Barragán went to Sacramento Solons spring-training camp in 1956 and was farmed out to the Amarillo Gold Sox. In 1957, Barragán caught 108 games for the Solons. When the Solons attempted to send him to the Atlanta Crackers, he instead retired from baseball. When the Portland Beavers came to town with both of their catchers injured, they signed Barragán, buying him from the Solons for $1. In 1960, Barragán hit .318 in 89 games for the Solons. (Courtesy of Cuno Barragán.)

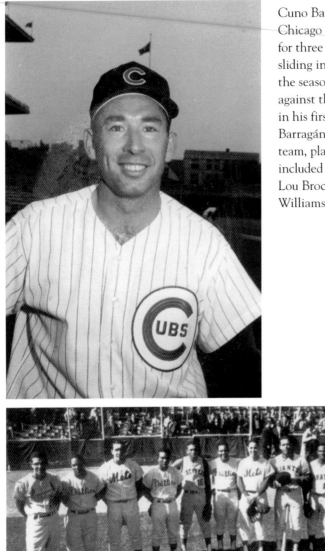

Cuno Barragán was drafted by the Chicago Cubs, and he played for the team for three years. In 1961, he broke his ankle sliding into third base and sat out most of the season. He got back into the lineup against the Giants and hit a home run in his first major-league at-bat. In 1962, Barragán had a good year on a bad Cubs team, playing in 59 games. His teammates included Richie Ashburn, Ernie Banks, Lou Brock, Al Heist, Ron Santo, and Billy Williams. (Courtesy of Cuno Barragán.)

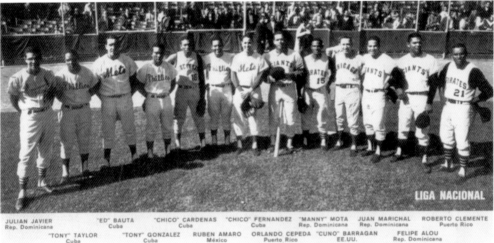

On October 12, 1963, the first and last Latin American All-Star Game was played at the Polo Grounds. The National League all-stars faced off against the American League all-stars. Players included Felipe Alou, Luis Aparicio, Orlando Cepeda, Roberto Clemente, Minnie Minoso, Juan Marichal, Manny Mota, Tony Oliva, Vic Power, and Diego Sequi. Marichal pitched and Cuno Barragán caught the entire game, which ended in a 5-2 National League win. This was the last game played at the Polo Grounds. (Courtesy of Cuno Barragán.)

The Mexican American Hall of Fame Sports Association (MAHFSA) is a nonprofit organization formed in 1973 to foster, encourage, promote, advance, and create interest in the practice and enjoyment of sport activities among the community's youth. The MAHFSA honors athletes who have distinguished themselves in the field of sports and have made community contributions in the Sacramento area. MAHFSA awards scholarships to high school senior athletes pursuing higher education. One of the first honorees in 1973 was Cuno Barragán, a local star player. (Courtesy of Cuno Barragán.)

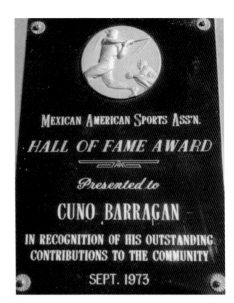

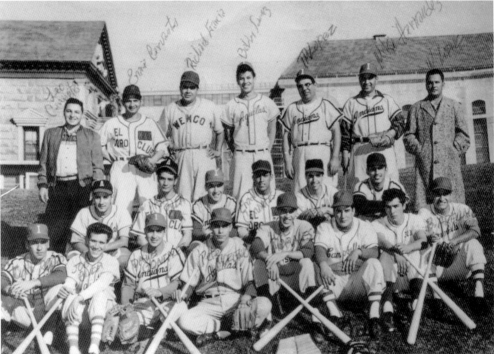

The 1958 Mexican American All-Star Team poses at Folsom Prison before playing the Represa Eagles. The Eagles included former minor-league and major-league players. Shown here are, from left to right, (first row) all-stars Tony Rojo, Joe Blea, Dave González, Lupe Moreno, three unidentified, and Ben Arellano; (second row) unidentified, Hank Blea, unidentified, Ernie Cervantes Jr., and two unidentified; (third row) Leo Cervantes, Ernie Cervantes Sr., Richard Garcia, Bobby Saenz, T.M. López, Mike Hernández, and W. López. (Courtesy of Mexican American Hall of Fame Sports Association.)

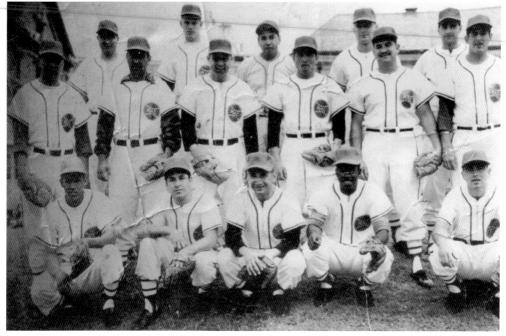

The 1958 Sacramento Mexican Athletic Club team poses at Folsom Prison, ready to play the Represa Eagles. Shown here are, from left to right, (first row) Ernie Cervantes Jr. (first MAC batboy), Tony Rojo, Corky Ramírez, unidentified, and Dick Alejo; (second row) Andy Campos, Mike Hernández, Pete Campos, Louie Contreras, Rudy Saenz, and Al Zúñiga; (third row) Tony Alvarado, Bob Shoemaker, Joe Moreno, Jim Fellos, and Joe Viega. (Courtesy of Mexican American Hall of Fame Sports Association.)

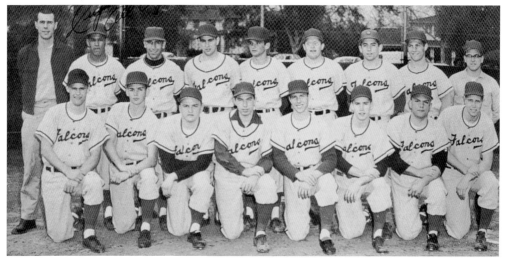

Gene Cervantes is one of the four baseball sons of Ernie Cervantes Sr.; the others are Ernie Jr., Eddie, and Eric. Gene was a key player on Sacramento's Bishop Armstrong (now Christian Brothers) Falcons baseball club that posted a 22-2 record in 1962. The Falcons boasted six all-city selections, including Gene, who hit a whopping .367 that year. Pictured in the second row, far left, is coach Dick Sperbeck; Gene is to the right of Sperbeck. (Courtesy of Christian Brothers High School.)

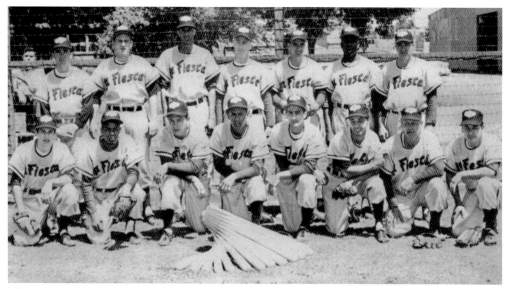

The 1966 La Fiesta team of the Sacramento County League gathers at Leiva Park. The players are from previous Sacramento MAC rosters and represent "B" team graduates, local college players, and a couple of MAC old-timers. Shown here are, from left to right, (first row) Ray Márquez, Norman Blackwell, unidentified, Ernie Cervantes Jr., Joe Viegas, Bobby Gonzalvez, unidentified, and Tony Rojo; (second row) Tom Higgins, Don Nanini, John Blackwell, unidentified, Chuck Lota, unidentified, and Tony Alverado. (Courtesy of Mexican American Hall of Fame Sports Association.)

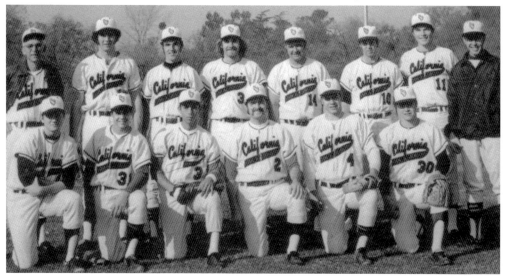

Ramón "Junior" Gonzáles starred at Sacramento City College, which won the 1971 Valley Conference championship. He excelled at Oregon State University and played in the Northwest League for the Seattle Rainiers. California Loan and Jewelry sponsored Sacramento teams, showcasing local professional players home during the off-season. Ramón is in the first row, fourth from the left. Bob Forsch, in the second row, second from right, pitched two no-hitters for the St. Louis Cardinals. (Mexican American Hall of Fame Sports Association.)

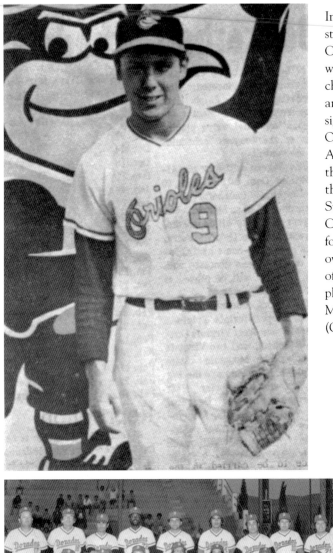

In 1971, Eddie Cervantes starred on the Sacramento City College team that won the Valley Conference championship; he was co-MVP and made all-conference. He signed with the Baltimore Orioles and was assigned to the Appalachian League. This was the beginning of seven years that took him to the Florida State, Northwest, and the California Leagues. He played for the Portland Mavericks, owned by Bing Russell, father of actor Kurt Russell. Cervantes played seven years in the Mexican professional leagues. (Courtesy of Eddie Cervantes.)

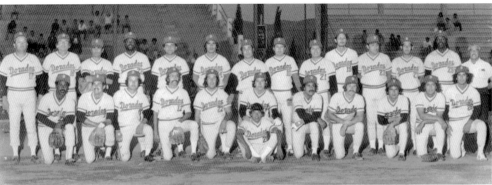

Released by the Atlanta Braves in 1976, Eric Cervantes tried out with the Chihuahua Dorados baseball team. His brother Eddie joined him, not realizing his contract was held by the Portland baseball club; both made the team. When the National Association of Professional Baseball Leagues realized the conflict in contracts, it ordered Eddie back to Portland. The brothers are shown in this team photograph: Eric is in the front row, far right, and Eddie is to the left of him. (Courtesy of Eddie Cervantes.)

SACRAMENTO

Eddie Cervantes returned to the Portland Mavericks. His contract was sold in 1977 to the Iowa Oaks, the Triple-A franchise of the Chicago White Sox. He asked for his release before the Sox optioned him out, and he rejoined his brother Eric in the Double-A Tabasco State League. Eddie was playing with the Macuspana Parrots when his contract was sold to the Nuevo Laredo Owls of the Mexican League. He is seen here before a game in Mexico City at the Estadio Seguro Social. (Courtesy of Eddie Cervantes.)

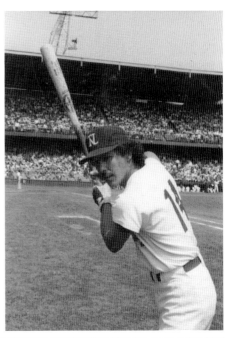

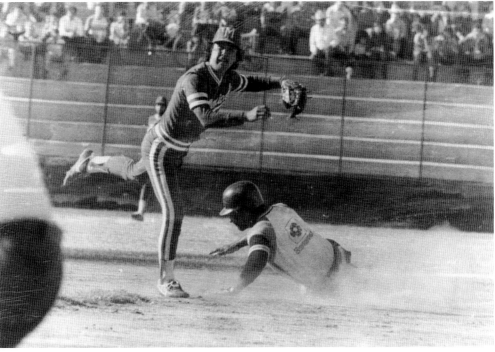

In 1979, Eddie Cervantes began a four-season stretch with the Mexicali Aguilas (Eagles) in Mexico's Pacific Coast Winter League. He played in one all-star game. Here, he is turning a double play. Known for his elegant style of defensive play, "Silky" also produced with the bat. On November 11, 1980, he hit a two-run home run in the bottom of the 20th inning to end what may still be the longest game in Mexican Winter League history. (Courtesy of Eddie Cervantes.)

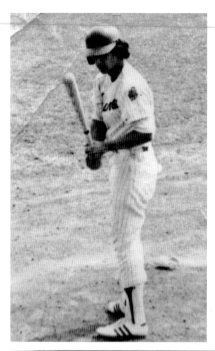

A 1974 graduate of Hiram Johnson High School in Sacramento, Eric Cervantes was an all-city baseball selection. He was picked in the ninth round by the Atlanta Braves. He is seen here in the on-deck circle for the Kingsport Braves (Atlanta Braves affiliate) before having the game of his career in which he hit for the cycle (single, double, triple, and home run) against the Pulaski Phillies (Philadelphia Phillies affiliate). He played for five seasons in Mexican professional baseball. (Courtesy of Eddie Cervantes.)

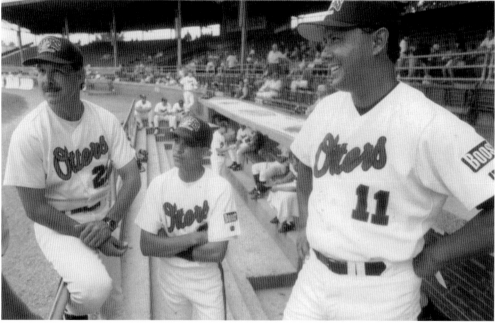

The Evansville Otters is an independent professional team in the Frontier League in Indiana. Seen here in 1996 are the manager, Fred "Fernando" Arroyo (left), and Eddie Cervantes (right), a coach. Fernando and Eddie played against each other in Little League, high school, and American Legion baseball in Sacramento and during their professional careers in Mexico. They are pictured at Bosse Field in Evansville, the stadium used for filming parts of the movie *A League of their Own*, the story of women's professional baseball during World War II. (Courtesy of Eddie Cervantes.)

SACRAMENTO

SAN GABRIEL VALLEY

The San Gabriel Valley lies to the east of Los Angeles, to the north of the Puente Hills, to the south of the San Gabriel Mountains, and west of the Inland Empire. It derives its name from the San Gabriel River, which flows through the center of the Valley. The river itself was named for the Spanish Mission San Gabriel Arcángel, which was built in Whittier Narrows in 1771. The mission served as the starting point for the original Spanish settlers' (Los Pobladores) nine-mile walk to Los Angeles in 1781 that initiated the founding of the city of Los Angeles.

For decades, the San Gabriel Valley's economy rested largely on agriculture and ranching. Besides cattle and crops, the region produced a variety of wines. The westward movement brought thousands of people into the Valley after the US Civil War. The economy expanded into manufacturing, packinghouses, railroads, foundries, oil fields, small businesses, and construction. Eventually, cities became incorporated in the early 1900s. There are 31 cities and five unincorporated neighborhoods in the San Gabriel Valley. The Valley has nearly two million residents, almost 20 percent of the population in Los Angeles County.

Most communities in the San Gabriel Valley continue to have significant Mexican American populations, including Azusa, Baldwin Park, City of Industry, Duarte, El Monte, Irwindale, La Puente, Montebello, Rosemead, South El Monte, West Covina, Whittier, and San Gabriel. It was largely in these neighborhoods that baseball took root. Mexican American baseball can be traced to at least the early 1900s in the Valley. As occurred elsewhere, baseball played important social and cultural roles in the development of these ethnic enclaves. Baseball allowed these otherwise isolated communities to be directly connected through a series of games and tournaments. Many Mexican American leaders received their first political lessons on the baseball diamond; moreover, baseball networks eventually promoted political organizations. Baseball was a safe haven where the Mexican culture and language was respected and encouraged.

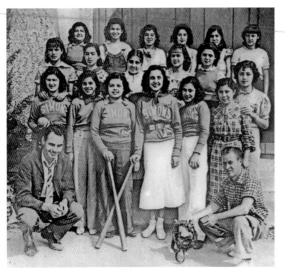

In 1905, Walter Simons, a wealthy industrialist from Iowa, chose a largely undeveloped area of East Los Angeles for the construction of a brickyard. This area eventually became the cities of Montebello and Commerce. This 1937 photograph shows the eighth-grade girls' baseball team at Vail School. Louise Romo (first row, fourth from left) was born in Hurley, New Mexico, in 1923. Other players include Dolores Mosqueda, Sara Vásquez, Victoria Díaz, Irene Prado, Sara Hernández, and Catuta Bejarano. (Courtesy of the Montebello Historical Society.)

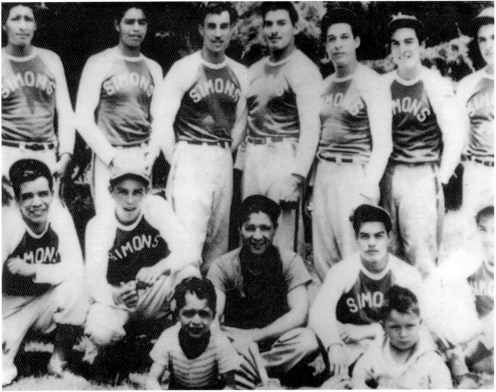

On this 1940s Simons team is David Contreras (first row, second from left), who married Rachel Romo. Other players include Ernie Villa (second row, third from left), Vincent Olague (first row, far left), Henry Rodelo (second row, fifth from left), Jesse García (first row, third from left), and Chuck González (second row, second from right). The two batboys are Nick Morales (left) and Ernie Contreras. Villa was a baseball and track star at Montebello High School. He served in World War II and Korea. (Courtesy of Linda Herrera.)

Tony Villa, Ernie's brother, was born in Montebello, California, in 1927. He played baseball between 1943 and 1951, competing during the week and on weekends. He was scouted by the major leagues. Villa married Dorothy Mae Webster in 1949, and they had four children: Michael, Ronnie, Kathy, and George. After baseball, Villa worked as a crane operator for 15 years and later as a carpenter for 27 years. His three boys and his grandchildren played baseball and softball. (Courtesy of Ronnie Villa.)

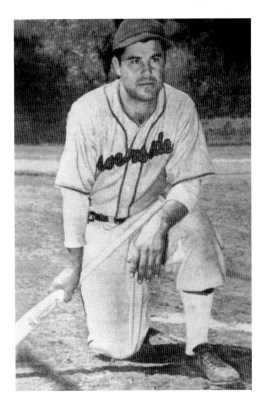

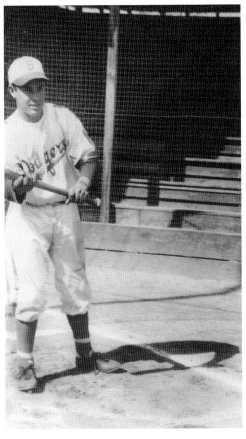

Tony Villa was signed by the Brooklyn Dodgers in 1946 and played for the Valdosta Dodgers in the Class D Georgia-Florida League. The following season, he played for the Zaneville Dodgers in the Ohio State League. In 1948, he was traded to the New York Yankees, playing one year in its minor-league system with the Bisbee-Douglas Miners of the Arizona-Texas League. Villa's last two years of professional baseball were in Riverside, California, with the Sunset League. (Courtesy of Ronnie Villa.)

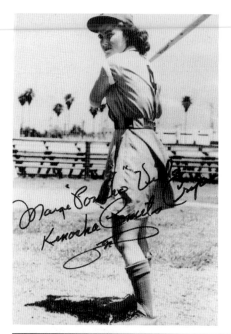

Marge Villa was an outstanding shortstop for several teams, including Montebello City, the Orange County Lionettes, and the California All-Stars. She was recruited by the All-American Girls Professional Baseball League and drafted in 1946 by the Wakesha Comets at the age of 21. She became one of the best catchers in the history of the Comets. The hometown crowds shouted "Viva Villa!" after each great play. At the age of 88, she throws batting practice for Little League teams. (Courtesy of Margaret Villa Cryan.)

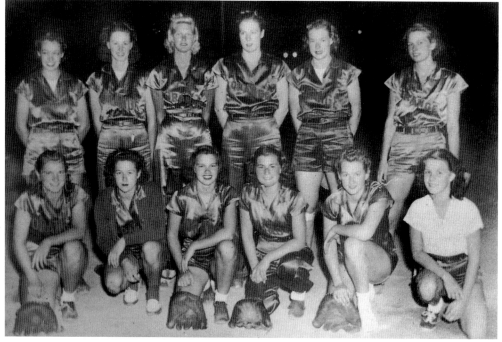

Marge Villa (first row, third from right) played for the Orange County Lionettes at the age of 16, the youngest on the team. She had been recruited at 14 by the Lionettes, but her mother thought that was too young to play ball with mature women. *The Los Angeles Times* ran a story in 1948 highlighting the 11 women from California who were recruited for the All-American Girls Professional Baseball League and included a photograph of Villa sliding into third base. (Courtesy of Margaret Villa Cryan.)

SAN GABRIEL VALLEY

Ronnie Villa played for the Montebello Little League in 1963. Like many of his generation, Ronnie had older family members who had played baseball and softball, serving as role models and later as coaches for their children. Ron's two brothers, Michael and George, played Little League and baseball at Cantwell High School. Ronnie's son Jay-Michael continues to play ball and coaches at California High School in Whittier. (Courtesy of Ronnie Villa.)

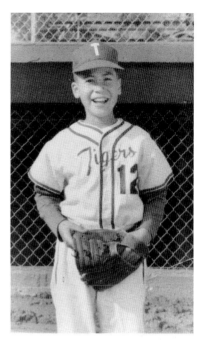

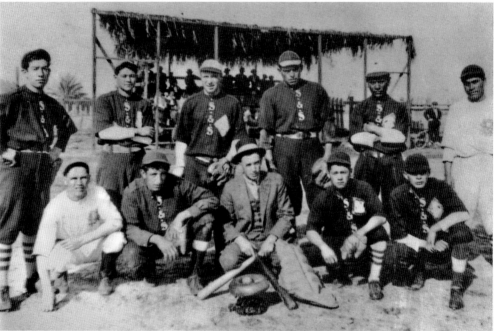

Manuel (De La Ossa) Henninger (first row, far right) was born in San Gabriel. He was known as "El Gato" (The Cat) because of his speed on the base paths. The "Henninger Flats" in the San Gabriel Mountains are named after his grandfather William Kimber Henninger. The 1915 San Gabriel team shown here includes Nacho Rangel, Ed Salcedo, Willie Acuña, and "Little Joe" and "Big Joe" Acuña. Slack and Salcido Brothers Groceries and Hardware Store sponsored the team, thus the double "S & S" on the jerseys. (Courtesy of James Henninger Aguirre.)

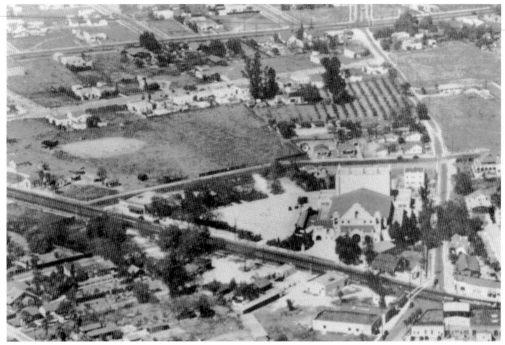

This 1933 aerial photograph shows the San Gabriel Mission District and the Mission Play House and surrounding neighborhood. The San Gabriel baseball diamond had been excavated by manager Mike Salazar at South Mission Drive, near the corner of Broadway Avenue. The field was home to outstanding teams and great players from the San Gabriel region. Several visiting teams from Mexico graced the field with their extraordinary play. (Courtesy of Camilia López.)

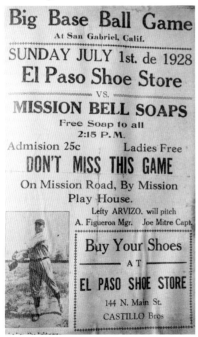

This is an advertisement for a game between El Paso Shoe Store and Mission Bell Soaps. Games were promoted by placing posters on storefront windows and telephone poles and in community centers, church halls, and theater lobbies. This particular poster announces a game in 1928 in San Gabriel. (Courtesy of Orozco family.)

EL PASO SHOES WIN

The El Paso Shoe nine thumped the San Gabriel club, 12 to 2, yesterday. Score:

EL PASO SHOES	AB	H	O	A	SAN GABRIEL	AB	H	O	A
Orosco,rf	6	3	1	1	Thorne,3b	4	0	1	0
Kat'ros,2b	5	1	3	0	Diaz,c	4	2	7	2
Lima,3b	4	2	2	2	Gonzales,lf	4	0	1	0
Speaker,ss	5	2	0	4	Perez,ss	3	1	1	2
M.Lopez,cf	4	1	2	0	Gradias,1b	4	1	11	1
E.Lopez,1b	4	1	8	0	M'All'er,2b	3	1	3	1
Rod'quez,p	3	2	0	0	Manzer,rf	4	3	1	0
Metro,c	5	2	10	2	Molina,cf	4	0	2	0
Ramirez,lf	5	0	1	0	Puter,p	1	1	0	1
					Ryan,p	1	0	0	2
					Vidales,lf	1	0	0	0
Totals	41	14	29	9	Totals	33	9	27	9

SCORE BY INNINGS

El Paso Shoes......4 0 2 1 5 0 0 0 0—12
Base hits ......4 0 3 2 4 0 0 0 1—14
San Gabriel ......0 1 0 0 0 0 0 1 0— 2
Base hits ......0 2 1 1 1 0 1 1 2— 9

SUMMARY

Errors—Speaker, Perez. Innings pitched —By Rodriguez, 9; Luter, 3 1-3; Ryan, 2 2-3; Cerez, 3. Credit victory to Rodriquez. Charge defeat to Puter. Struck out—By Rodriquez, 8; Perez, 4. Hit by pitched ball—Speaker. Stolen bases—Orozco, Ramirez. Three-base hit—Orozco. Time of game—2h.

Major Los Angeles newspapers ran stories on community baseball throughout the region, including Mexican American teams such as El Paso Shoe Store, San Fernando Merchants, Carmelita Provisions Company, and several others. The papers included game summaries, box scores, and side notes. This is a box score of a game between El Paso and a San Gabriel team in the late 1920s. Fans purchased newspapers to keep abreast of their favorite neighborhood teams. (Courtesy of the Orozco family.)

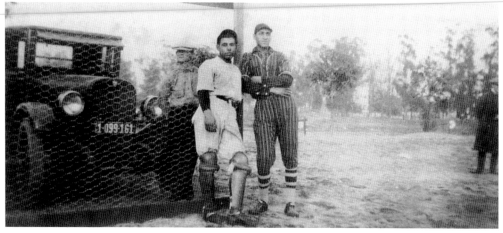

After California gained independence from Mexico, the governor, Pío Pico, sold the 21 missions in 1846. Pres. Abraham Lincoln returned the missions to the Catholic Church. Mexican American teams played their games around the mission. Here, players Andrés Díaz (left) and Joe Barreras pose before a game. The car and the well-dressed man to the right indicate that wealthy and influential people attended games, contrary to the notion that Mexican American baseball attracted only working-class fans. (Courtesy of Margaret Sosa.)

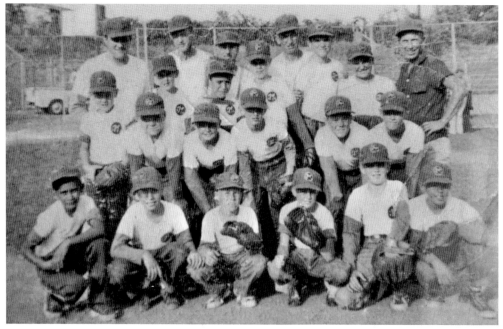

Fertile lands, as well as ample water within local boundaries, inspired San Gabriel's early agricultural focus. Significant numbers of Mexican Americans were employed by local ranchers and farmers, while others worked in the packinghouses and with the railroads. Since then, generations of Mexican Americans have played ball, especially youths. The Tigers of San Gabriel were proclaimed champions of the American Minor League in 1954, winning 17 of 18 regular-season games and both playoff games.

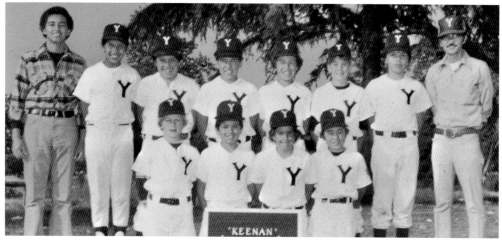

The 1979 Keenan Little League Yankees of La Puente were the first-half winners. Shown here are, from left to right, (first row) Kelly Segal, Ray Ramírez, James King, and Steven Akiyoshi; (second row) coach Orlando Gonzáles, Raúl Mendoza, Robbie Fregoso, Mario Félix, Ernie Ceyela, Sam Manning, James Henninger Aguirre, and coach Christ Akiyoshi. Aguirre, born in San Gabriel, was the first pick of the La Puente Major League Yankees as a pitcher and catcher. (Courtesy of James Henninger Aguirre.)

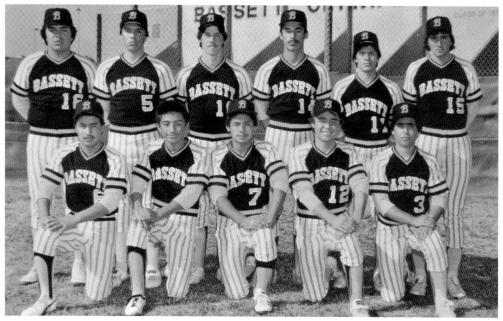

James Henninger Aguirre was a standout pitcher for the 1984 Bassett Olympians high school team. Like his grandfather Manuel, James could bring the "heat" with his fiery fastball. Shown here are, from left to right, (first row) Steve Chávez, William Hernández, Martín Martínez, Jack Vigil, and Manuel Martines; (second row) Eddie Hidalgo, Aguirre, Dean Ramos, Andy Lucero, Román Gardea, and coach Nick Janis. The season was dedicated to former standout pitcher Adrián Barraza. (Courtesy of James Henninger Aguirre.)

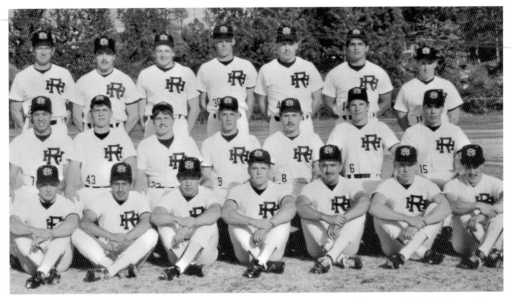

The Rio Hondo Community College Roadrunners team is seen here in 1985. The college, located in Whittier, California, draws outstanding baseball and softball players from surrounding communities, including Whittier, Pico Rivera, Santa Fe Springs, El Monte, and South El Monte. James Henninger Aguirre (second row, far right) was the only walk-on pitcher to make the team. Other players included Ralph Acosta, Anthony Corona, Kiki García, Tim Jiménez, Dan Elías, Steve Muñoz, and Rudy Martínez. (Courtesy of James Henninger Aguirre.)

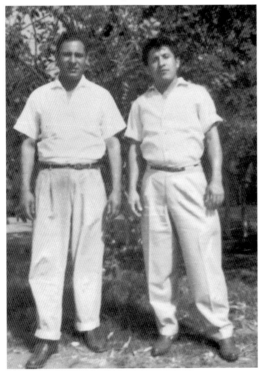

José Francisco Acosta was born in Texas and served in World War II before moving to Los Angeles and working for the Southern Pacific Railroad. Acosta (left) and his best friend and teammate Chico López stayed friends for their entire lives. The players dressed in the same attire to attend team-sponsored events. This photograph was taken around 1958 at Lincoln Park in East Los Angeles. Acosta often commented that these were the happiest times in his life. (Courtesy of Nancy Acosta Delira.)

SAN GABRIEL VALLEY

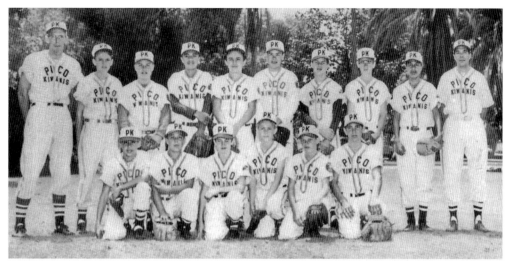

The Pico Kiwanis team was managed by Abelino Andujo. Gene Pico (second row, second from right) played third base and shortstop and made the all-star team, winning the batting championship in 1951 at Friends Park. Pico loved baseball so much that he found time to play in several leagues in Montebello, Pasadena, and Maywood that year. He said that it was a great experience playing in different leagues against other players in order to compare one's abilities and skills. (Courtesy of Gene Pico.)

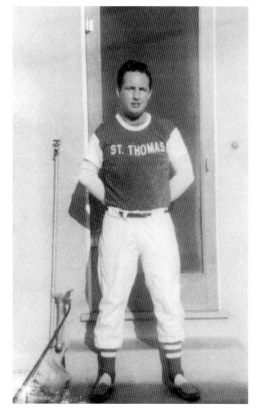

Bert Verdugo, uncle of Gene Pico, can trace his family roots to the Verdugos, a prominent California family. He attended school in the Mexican community known as "Jimtown" in Whittier. Besides softball, Verdugo wrestled at Whittier Union High. He played for Culver City, Downey Merchants, Downey Impalas, Lakewood Jets, Los Alamitos, and First Security Investment. Verdugo played on the same team as his sons, Danny and Marty, and has been a role model to his grandchildren and great-grandchildren. (Courtesy of Bert Verdugo.)

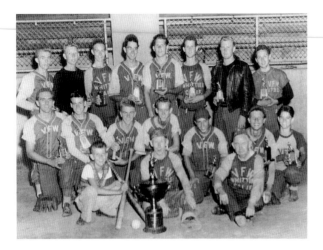

Bert Verdugo (standing, far right) took his VFW teams to national tournaments two years in a row. In 1947, his team finished second, but it captured the championship the following season. Verdugo won numerous awards during his softball career, and he once pitched 49 innings in a tournament. He pitched in senior tournaments until he tore a muscle in his left arm, ending his career at the age of 68. (Courtesy of Bert Verdugo.)

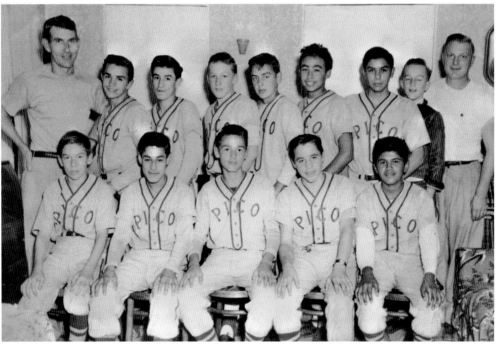

The 1951 Pico Rivera Little League Pirates are shown after completing their San Gabriel Valley Fall League schedule. They are, from left to right, (first row) Ronald Barlass, Art Lagunas, Joe Hunt, Dick Constable, and David Olague; (second row) coach Art Barlass, Frank Colantuano, Bob Lagunas, Barton Kirk, Carl Clayton, David Salazar, Julian Barry Aguirre, Mike Hamlin, and coach Harris O. Hogenson. Bob and Art Lagunas were outstanding players in high school, community college, state college, and on military teams. (Courtesy of James Henninger Aguirre.)

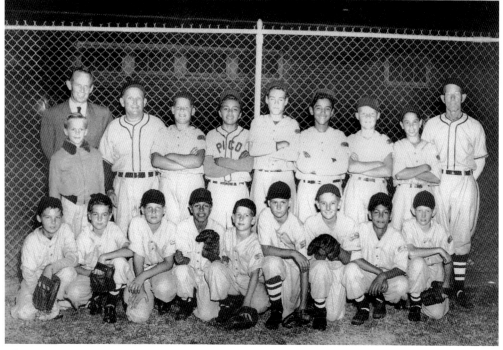

The 1950–1951 Little League team played its games at Friends Park in Whittier. Gene Pico (first row, fourth from left) was an outstanding hitter, twice making the all-star team. His older brothers, cousins, and uncles played baseball and softball in Whittier and in the area now known as Pico Rivera. Gene's great-great-grandfather Pio Pico was the last governor of California under Mexican rule. His mother's side of the family are the Verdugos, another prominent California clan. (Courtesy of Gene Pico.)

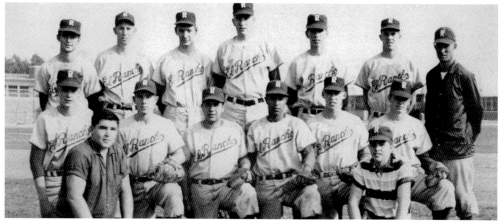

Gene Pico (second row, fourth from left) played varsity baseball at El Rancho High School in Pico Rivera in the 1950s. He made all-league all three years of ball and still found time to play in the Los Angeles Municipal League. He also played ball at Cerritos Community College in Norwalk, California. Pico left school and turned down a major-league contract with the Dodgers to support his family. He plays senior softball at the age of 73. (Courtesy of Gene Pico.)

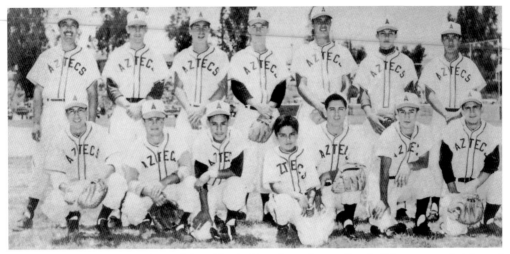

The Pico Aztecs were members of the 1954 Golden State Senior Baseball League, with Manuel Moreno as manager. The league was loaded with talent, with players from all-city and California Interscholastic Federation (CIF) teams. The Aztecs were led by players like Willie García from Wilson, Vince Zeims from Franklin, and Conrad Muñatones from Roosevelt. Bobby Moreno and the Lagunas brothers, Art and Bob, played on El Rancho High School's first CIF playoff team, losing the championship game. (Courtesy of Bob Lagunas.)

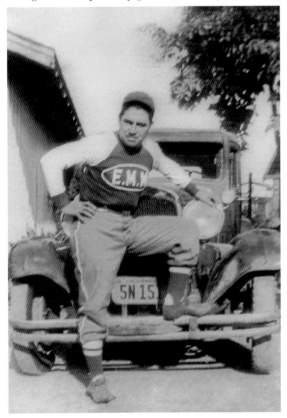

Manuel P. Venegas was raised in Medina Court in El Monte. He played for the El Monte Merchants. His love for the game led him to be a player, coach, manager, umpire, and announcer. As a catcher, Manuel threw out runners from his knees and was respected and feared by opposing teams for his overall knowledge of the game. His teams won many championships in softball and baseball. Most of his seven sons played ball. (Courtesy of Ronald W. Venegas.)

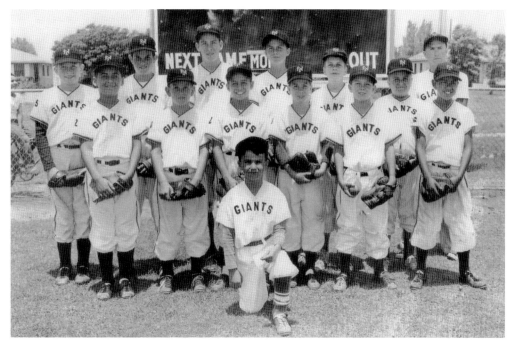

The Norwood Village National Little League was born in 1954 with a handful of Mexican American players. Ronald W. Venegas is in the second row, far right; Phillip García is in the first row, far left; the batboy is Mike Barrios. García went on to be a college professor, and Barrios later served on the El Monte City Council. Venegas batted .340 for the season but was denied a spot on the all-star team. Many believed that the slight was due to lingering racial prejudice. (Courtesy of Ronald W. Venegas.)

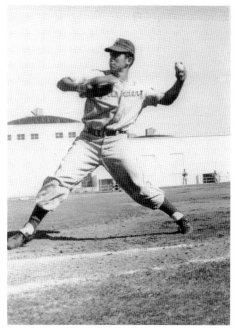

Manuel Venegas Jr. played first base at Pasadena City College in 1960. He injured his knee sliding into second base, requiring surgery that ended his dream of playing baseball at the University of Southern California. He still attended USC and was the first person from Medina Court to graduate from that campus. He became an electrical engineer but, sadly, was killed in a car accident at the age of 28 in 1968. (Courtesy of Ronald W. Venegas.)

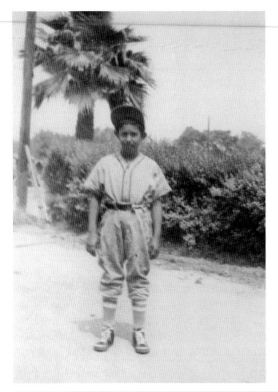

Manuel Venegas Jr. is seen here at the age of eight in 1948 in Medina Court. The elder Venegas had other ball-playing sons: Robert, who played at Arroyo High School and Citrus Junior College; Camilo, who played Little League; Ronald, who played Little League and Pony League; and Joseph, who played Little League and Babe Ruth League. Most of Manuel Sr.'s sons played football and other sports in the neighborhood and in school. (Courtesy of Ronald W. Venegas.)

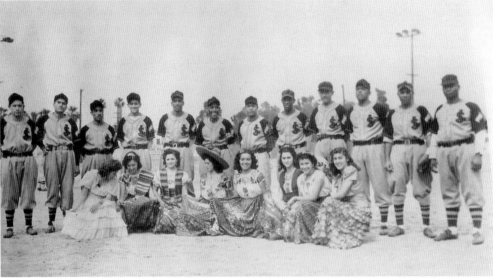

This photograph shows a Cuban team playing in Baldwin Park around 1932. The folklórico dance group, known as the Princesses, was comprised of local young women. Natividad Rodríguez (first row, third from left) married Ben Quiroz, a prominent rancher in the San Gabriel Valley. Virginia Castruita (first row, fourth from right) was the daughter of Max Castruita, one of the pioneering families that settled in the farming camp of Medina Court in El Monte in 1910. (Courtesy of the Linda Quiroz Archives.)

John Hernández holds his Irwindale Sabres fast-pitch senior jersey. He played youth ball and softball in the military and was a member of the 1959 Irwindale Clovers. The Clovers played teams from Chino, Azusa, La Puente, Basset, Baldwin Park, La Verne, El Monte, San Gabriel, Pomona, and Gardena. Manager Ben Aguayo made the 1959 Clovers exceptionally talented. The players on that team included Art Tapia Jr., Gil Díaz, Joe Moctezuma, Arnold Medina, Albert Moreno, Bobby Fraijo, and the Chico clan of John, Edward, David, Bobby, and Víctor. (Courtesy of John Hernández.)

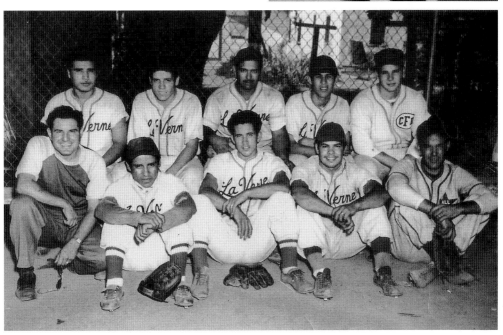

Paco Castellano coached the 1950s La Verne team, which played ball in high school and continued after graduation. When the Korean War broke out in 1950, some players went into the service, including David Rodríguez. Jess Mora was good enough to play professional ball, but he was not given a fair chance due to racial discrimination. Members of the team eventually married local girls and worked in various jobs. Other players included Tommie Encinas, Johnny Carmona, Henry Saldivar, and Ron Renike. (Courtesy of Dennis Duke Romo.)

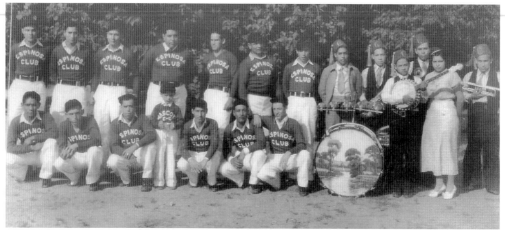

This 1934 photograph shows both the Monrovia Espinosa Baseball Club and the Johnny Luna Band. The ballplayers are, from left to right, (first row) Martín Cabrera, Joe Ramos, Joe Acuña, Jimmy Espinosa Jr. (team founder's son), Gavino Luera, Claro Olivas, and Ralph Muñoz; (second row) Jesse Bracamonte, Mike Miranda, Ralph Guardado, Jim Espinosa (team founder), Eugenio Muñoz, Ralph Hernández, and Alex Dávalos. Bracamonte also played for 20 years with the Monrovia Merchants, starting in 1933. (Courtesy of Víctor Guardado.)

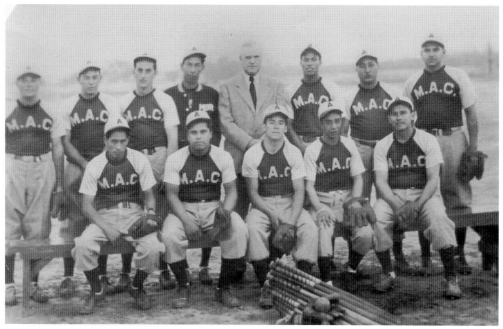

Henry Toledo was born in Azusa. He and his two brothers, Manuel and Lawrence, were gifted athletes. In high school, Henry lettered in five sports: baseball, football, basketball, track, and tennis. Manuel organized the Mexican American Club that sponsored sports teams from Azusa. He built the baseball field, including the bleachers, arranged schedules with local teams, found sponsors, and solicited local merchants for equipment. Manuel (not shown) was the manager of this team, and Henry (first row, far left) played second base. (Courtesy of Henry Toledo.)

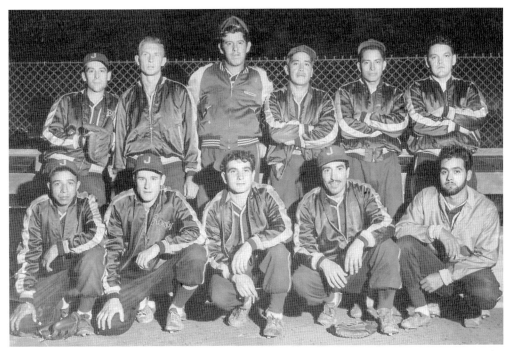

Henry Toledo joined the Marine Corps before the attack on Pearl Harbor. He saw action in the South Pacific, earning 14 ribbons and medals and achieving the rank of officer. When he returned home, he played with his brother Manuel's Azusa team. Henry is seen here in the second row, second from the right. He joined the Army in 1951 and went to Korea, where he played on the baseball and basketball teams. Later, he worked at the Howard Hughes Company as an engineer on the 1969 moon landing. He coached his two sons, Floyd and Roy. (Courtesy of Henry Toledo.)

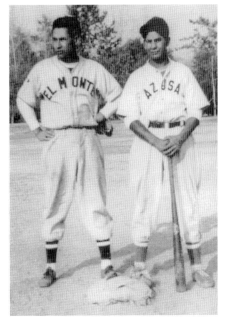

Fidel Soliz (right) was raised in the segregated community of Hicks Camp in El Monte. Manuel Torres (left) is wearing the El Monte uniform. Soliz played baseball with his brother Ramón. The Glendale Dodgers sent out a pickup truck to bring prospective players to games. This is the way that Soliz met Jackie Robinson. The two became good friends, and Robinson recruited Soliz to the Negro Leagues for a short time. Soliz played ball for the Navy during World War II. (Courtesy of Lucy Vera Pedregon.)

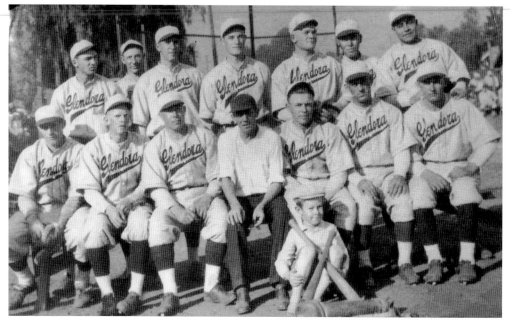

David Salazar (second row, far right), an outstanding player during the 1920s and 1930s, was recruited by the best teams, including this one from Glendora. His brother Mike owned land in San Gabriel; the family built a baseball diamond there. David is the grandfather of Darrell Evans, who played in the major leagues from 1969 to 1989. David's nephew Ernesto was a fine pitcher who dueled against Satchel Paige during weekend games at Griffith Park in Los Angeles. (Courtesy of the Orozco family.)

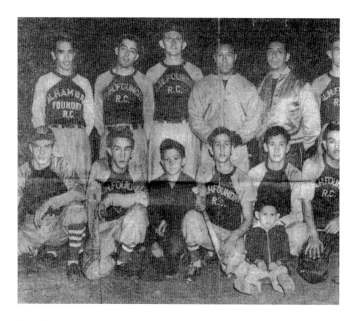

This 1950s Alhambra Foundry R.C. (Recreational Club) was comprised largely of Mexican Americans who worked at the Alhambra plant but lived in several surrounding communities, including San Gabriel, Rosemead, East Los Angeles, El Monte, La Puente, and Montebello. Players included Frank Félix, manager Joe Valdés, Tom Mata, Jack Feliz, Joe Bueno, Al Galindo, Richard Misguez, and Tommy Mata Jr. as batboy.

SAN GABRIEL VALLEY

6

INLAND EMPIRE

At the turn of the 20th century, the inland region of Southern California, more commonly known as the Inland Empire, sustained a thriving citrus industry that provided the economic incentive for Mexican immigration into the San Bernardino Valley, the Pomona Valley, Riverside, Corona, and as far as Calexico and the Coachella Valley. Mexican immigrants labored within the citrus economy as pickers, packers, and in other low-wage positions. Various Santa Fe and Southern Pacific railroad depots throughout the Inland Empire provided Mexican immigrants with additional employment. With the large influx of Mexican immigration during the first decades of the 20th century, long-lasting Mexican communities developed in the region. As migrants settled in Inland Empire barrios, Mexican immigrants and their Mexican American progeny formed baseball teams that facilitated growing senses of community pride and ethnic identity for men and women. Many of the barrio baseball games were played on weekend afternoons to lively and overflowing crowds. Some fans parked their cars in the outfield and blared their horns at every home run.

Both women and men formed community teams that allowed Mexican Americans to proclaim their social equality through athletic competition and to publicly demonstrate community strength. Mexican Americans utilized baseball as public forums to make gains in civil rights and raise awareness about recreational segregation and its affects on juvenile delinquency. Mexican American businesses, employers, and the Catholic Church sponsored many teams within the community and reinforced senses of cultural and ethnic pride. Many players went on to participate in their community as members of the League of United Latin American Citizens (LULAC) and Community Service Organization (CSO) and as the first Mexican American teachers in their school districts.

The sport also gave families an important space in which to unify fathers, sons, brothers, daughters, and grandsons. Baseball has proven to be an intergenerational sport, as many generations of families maintain active involvement in the game. Several players went on to compete in the major leagues. This chapter is a tribute to the stories and strength of former and current players that continue the legacies of Mexican American baseball.

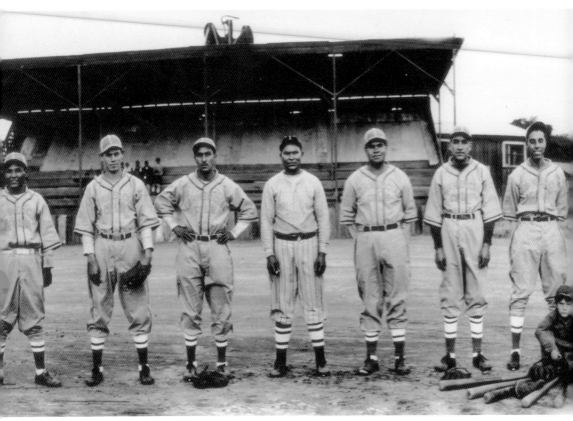

The San Bernardino–Colton Commercial Club poses at Cubs Park, also known as "El Corralón" (the Corral), in South Colton in November 1936. Owned by entrepreneur and team sponsor Juan Caldera, El Corralón served as a multipurpose recreational site for Mexican Americans in Colton.

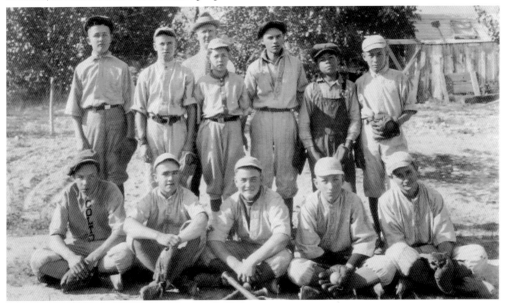

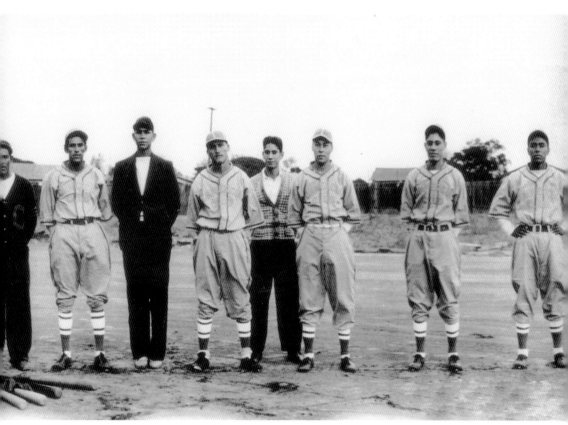

It had a community swimming pool, boxing facilities, and a baseball diamond. El Corralón proved to be especially important during this era, as Mexican Americans were segregated from Anglo recreational sites.

Opposite page: Pio Castorena (second row, second from right) played baseball as a child and well into his adult years. This photograph shows the Colton High School team from the 1920s. Like many immigrant families, the Castorenas experienced economic hardship and could not afford a high school uniform for Pio. He made the team, though, and showcased his talent for the Colton High School Yellowjackets. Pio eventually experienced teasing by players for not being able to afford shoes and for occasionally playing barefoot. (Courtesy of Rudy Castorena.)

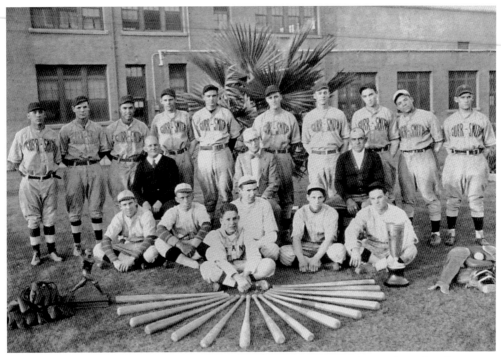

The Santa Fe Railroad was a main source of employment in San Bernardino. Pio Castorena eventually dropped out of high school to work for the railroad to help out his family. He (third row, second from right) and his brother Salvador (third row, third from the left) pose in this 1929 photograph. The brothers worked for the Santa Fe Railroad and played for the railroad's baseball team during the 1920s. (Courtesy of Rudy Castorena.)

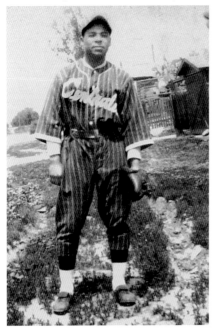

Pio Castorena poses in his San Bernardino-Colton Centrals uniform near his home in the South Colton barrio off of M Street in the early 1930s. Pio was known as a hustling and talented third baseman who eventually had a tryout with the Chicago White Sox. The San Bernardino Centrals featured talent from throughout the San Bernardino Valley. During the first few decades of the 20th century, a community of Mexicans and Mexican Americans emerged in south Colton in what became known as the "La Paloma" barrio. Many of the jobs for Mexicans in south Colton included working at either the nearby Southern Pacific or Santa Fe railroad depots. Colton later became a powerhouse for baseball in Southern California with the famous Colton Mercuries teams and produced a pioneering major-league baseball player in Camilo Carreon. (Courtesy of Rudy Castorena.)

INLAND EMPIRE

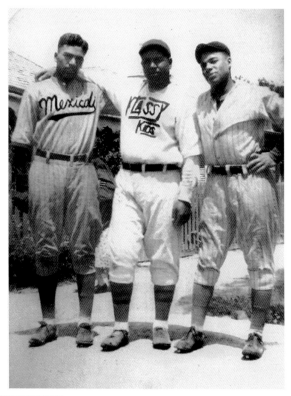

Baseball served as a unifier for Mexican families. Pio Castorena is shown at left with his brothers outside of their home in Colton. Salvador (far left) is wearing a Mexicali uniform. Many Mexicans during this time retained cultural roots and played for teams in Mexican leagues in places like Mexicali. Porfirio (center) is wearing a Klassy Kids uniform. Below, Pio demonstrates his stance on how to field a ball outside of his home in Colton. (Courtesy of Rudy Castorena.)

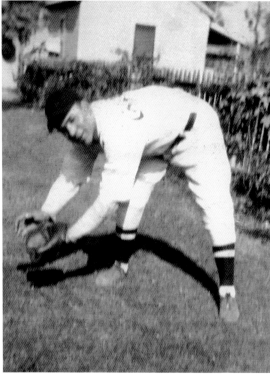

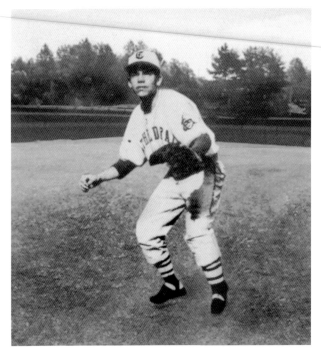

Pio Castorena's son Rudy is seen here in his Cathedral High School baseball uniform. Rudy, like Pio, was involved in baseball at an early age, playing for Resurrection Catholic Grammar School in Los Angeles. He attended Cathedral High School from 1957 through 1960, playing all four years in the outfield on a team comprised of predominantly Mexican American players. After high school, Rudy was a carpenter for 46 years and was a member of the Carpenters Union Local 1052. (Courtesy of Rudy Castorena.)

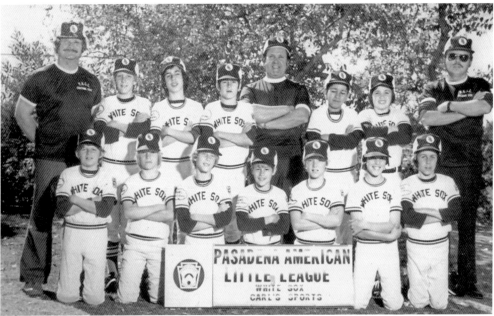

The 1977 Pasadena American Little League White Sox pose for a team photograph, which included Pio Castorena's grandson John Ramos (second row, third from right). Robert Seidler (first row, fourth from left) is the grandson of Walter O'Malley, the former owner of the Brooklyn and Los Angeles Dodgers. Seidler's brothers, Peter and Tommy, are majority owners of the San Diego Padres. Ramos has played in the Los Angeles Baseball League for the past 17 years. (Courtesy of John Ramos.)

INLAND EMPIRE

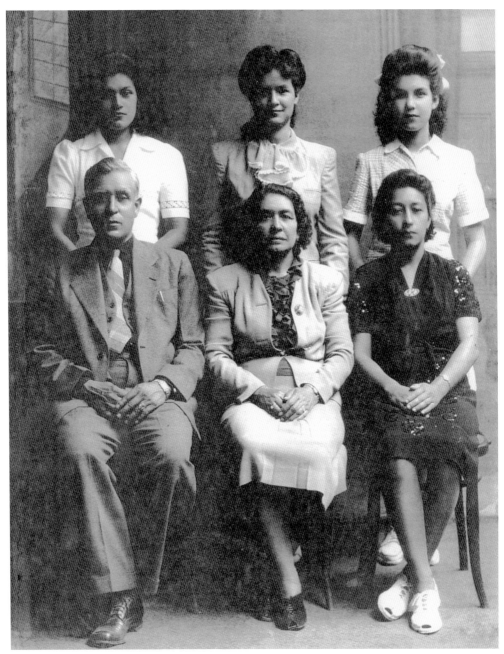

The Mitla Café proved critical in promoting Mexican cultural life in San Bernardino. Founded in 1937, the café was built on founder Lucia Rodríguez's gifts for crafting traditional Mexican food. Lucia and her daughters proved to be instrumental to the family's success, running the restaurant as the main cooks and waitstaff. Lucia's husband, Salvador, became involved in sponsoring local Mexican baseball and fast-pitch softball teams, many of which went on to win city league championships during the 1940s. Lucia (first row, center) is shown in this family portrait with her daughters and her husband. (Courtesy of Steve Oquendo.)

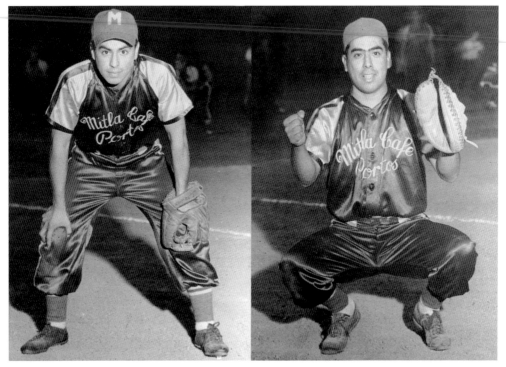

Baseball served as a family unifier for many Mexican Americans in the Inland Empire. The Botello brothers of San Bernardino played for the championship Mitla Café fast-pitch softball teams during the 1940s. In the photograph above, wearing their 1940s Mitla Café uniforms, are Lin (left) and Ralph. Below, Joe Botello is seen in his playing days. At right, he holds the 1940s Mitla Café uniform at an event celebrating the release of Arcadia's *Mexican American Baseball in the Inland Empire* at the historic Mitla Café in August 2012. The Botello family has a legacy of military service, and many of the Botello brothers proudly served in the US armed forces. (Courtesy of Mario Montecino and Joe Botello.)

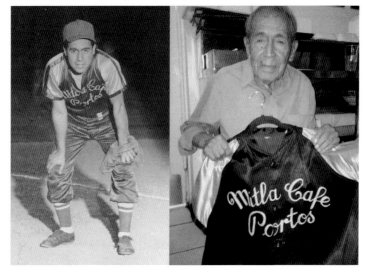

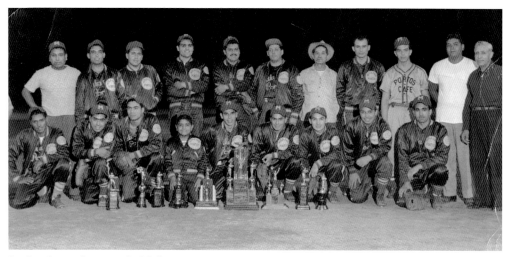

In the above photograph, Mitla Café city champions pose in 1949. From left to right are (first row) Bob Mancha, Ralph Botello, Speedy López, unidentified batboy, Larry Trujillo, Lin Botello, John Mejia, Joe Castanon, and Sal Rodríguez Jr.; (second row) manager Chevo Martínez, Cruz Nevarez, Joe Botello, Raúl Adame, Eliscio Adame, Juan González, Luz Negrete (scorekeeper), Fred Arce, Art Zumido, Mike Martínez (comanager), and Sal Rodríguez Sr. Nevarez's life demonstrates how baseball cultivated organizational and leadership skills. Despite living in an era of segregation and discrimination, Nevarez proudly served in the US Army during World War II, became one of San Bernardino's first Mexican American schoolteachers, and founded San Bernardino's chapter of the CSO. During the 1950s, a young Cesar Chávez worked with Nevarez in San Bernardino prior to his involvement with the United Farm Workers. Nevarez is seen at right as his students remember him: teaching a Spanish course at San Bernardino High School around 1955. (Courtesy of Carmen Domínguez Nevarez.)

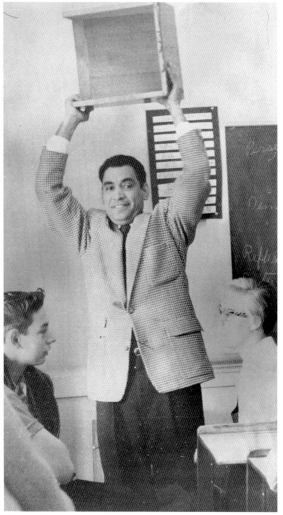

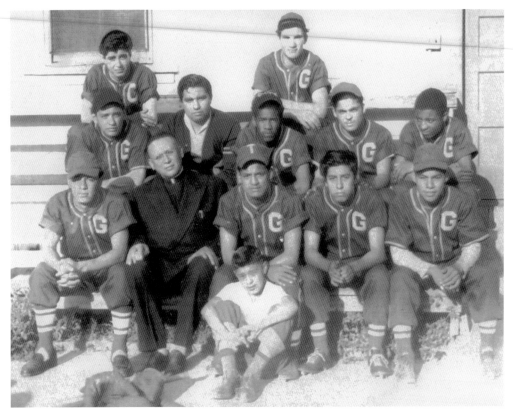

Church sponsorship was crucial for the development of Mexican American teams. Above, Fr. Jose Nuñez of Our Lady of Guadalupe Catholic Church, on the west side of San Bernardino, poses with his church-sponsored Guadalupe Angels team. Combating delinquency among Mexican youth was one of Padre Nuñez's primary objectives for the Mount Vernon barrio. Nuñez encouraged baseball, as it promoted solidarity and leadership skills. It proved to be an integral political space for Mexican Americans in San Bernardino, as Nuñez, Tommy Richardson (member of San Bernardino's city parks and recreation department), and other west-side community leaders initiated a successful court case against the City of San Bernardino to desegregate parks and recreational facilities for Mexicans in 1944. Tommy Richardson (not shown) managed this west-side team, known as the Mount Vernon White Sox, around 1945. (Courtesy of Felix Olguin.)

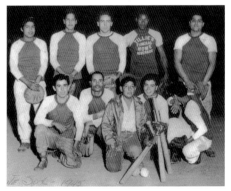

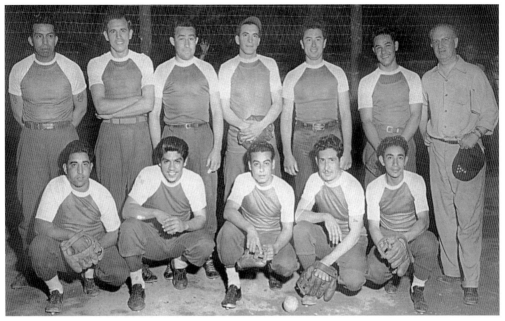

The 1946 Casa Blanca Stars pose at Emerald Street in Riverside's historic Casa Blanca barrio. From left to right are (first row) Tom Magdaleno, Tony Gomez, Amador Pacheco, Sylvester Aguilar, and Alex Benzor; (second row) Johnny Marquez, Manual Galvan, Jerome German, Frank Martinez, David Gualarte, Ernie Benzor, and M.B. Madden (manager). The Stars played clubs from San Bernardino, Corona, and Ontario. Benzor and his teammates wore their military belts to show they were deserving of civil rights. (Courtesy of Ernie Benzor Jr.)

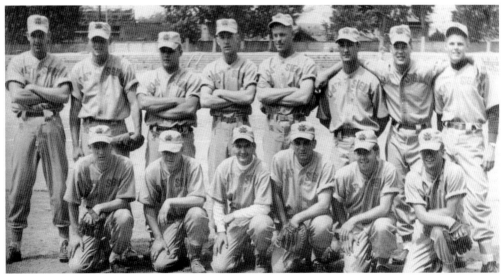

The 1939 Corona Athletics featured players like Ray Delgadillo and Tito Cortez. Delgadillo, Cortez, and Remi Chagnon eventually played for major-league farm teams. Carlos Uribe, one of the Athletics' most celebrated players, served in the Korean War. He is shown here in Korea (second row, third from right) with the 304th Signal Corps Battalion team in 1952.

Uniform Player Contract

APPROVED BY THE

NATIONAL ASSOCIATION

OF

PROFESSIONAL BASEBALL LEAGUES

IMPORTANT NOTICES

The attention of both Club and Player is specifically directed to the following excerpt from Rule 3 (a), of the Major-Minor League Rules:

"No Club shall make a contract different from the uniform contract and no club shall make a contract containing a non-reserve clause, except permission be first secured from the . . . President of the National Association. The making of any agreement between a Club and Player not embodied in the contract shall subject both parties to discipline."

A copy of this contract when executed must be delivered to player either in person or by registered mail, return receipt requested.

WAIVER OF SELECTION RIGHTS

I, the undersigned, the player party to the within contract, do hereby waive my right to have this contract selected by a Major League Club in the year 195_____, to the extent provided in Major-Minor Rule 5(g).

Date_____   _____
                                              Player's signature here in his OWN handwriting

NOTE — Major-Minor Rule 5 (g) reads as follows:

"Players of Open Classification clubs, who are subject to selection, in each contract they sign with an Open Classification club, may waive their first selection rights, and such contracts shall not be subject to selection; provided, however, that if assigned to a National Association club of lower classification, such assigned contracts shall be subject to selection under the rules applicable to the assignee club unless reassigned the same season to an Open Classification club; and provided, further, that if any such contract is assigned to a club of lower classification, the player shall be guaranteed all the compensation and considerations stipulated in his assigned contract unless unconditionally released."

CLUB FILL IN BELOW (TYPE OR PRINT)

CHUEY MENDOZA   TURSON
            PLAYER   CLUB

The Inland Empire produced standout baseball players, such as San Bernardino's Chuey Mendoza and Colton's Camilo Carreon. Mendoza played for the 1948 championship La Cabaña team from San Bernardino's west side. This team featured players like Ray Perez, Joe Delgado, Larry Trujillo, Richard Negrete, Lalo Bettencourt, Richard Casillas, Tony Cano, Manuel Leon, Morrison Aguila, and Sal Saavedra. Shown here is a contract that Mendoza signed with the Pacific Coast League's Seattle Rainiers' minor-league farm team based in Tucson; it was signed in 1952.

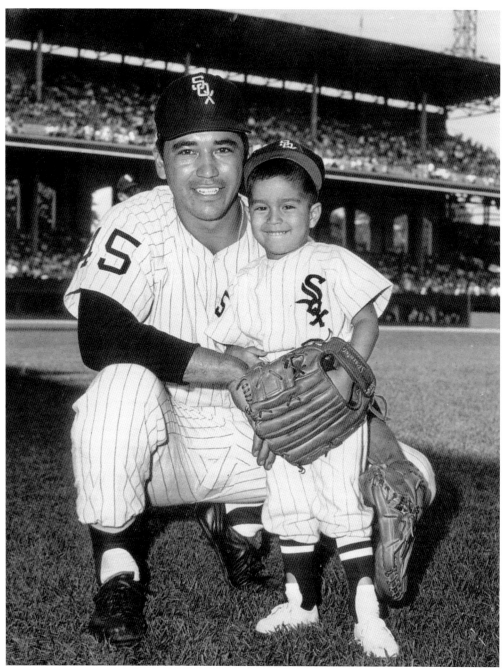

Upon graduation from Colton High School in 1956, Camilo Carreon signed with the Chicago White Sox organization. Playing for the Triple-A Indianapolis Indians of the American Association in 1959, Camilo hit .311 and earned Rookie of the Year honors. In nine minor-league seasons, he played in 694 games, compiling career totals of 29 home runs, 99 doubles, 17 triples, 189 RBI, and a .282 batting average; Camilo also played eight seasons in the majors. Camilo's son Mark Carreon also had a lengthy major-league career. (Courtesy of Pete Carrasco.)

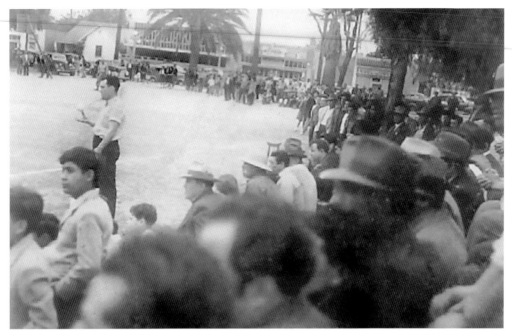

Games played at Seventh Street and Mount Vernon Avenue in San Bernardino drew thousands of fans on any given day. Enthusiastic supporters arrived early and lined the outfield with their cars in order to secure the best view. When players launched home runs, these fans honked their horns in celebration. In the above photograph, taken around 1945, an unnamed team takes the field as spectators from the San Bernardino barrio look on. The photograph below shows the patch for the legendary Mitla Café Portos teams of the late 1940s.

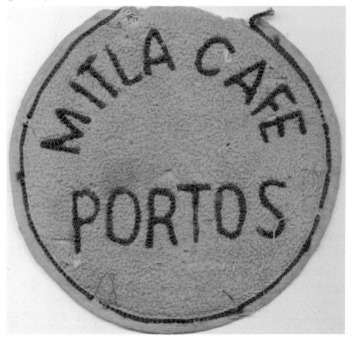

Joe Andrade, at right, was one of the best baseball players in Calexico's history. Born in Mexico, Andrade migrated with his family to Calexico and lived there until he was 18 years old. Andrade was a standout athlete his entire life; however, his dark skin complexion and the racial restrictions during the time held him back from becoming a professional. El Centro won this game 12-3 against the Flagstaff, Arizona, team during the Six States Semi-Pro Baseball Tournament in 1937. Below, he (first row, far left) poses with a team comprised of servicemen at Camp Ritchie in Maryland. Andrade, a Marine, fought in World War II. He and his fellow servicemen had just returned from fighting in 1945 when he put together a softball team. The reason the team competed in softball was because some players could not yet play hardball due to war wounds. (Courtesy of Rosemary Andrade and Steve Binder.)

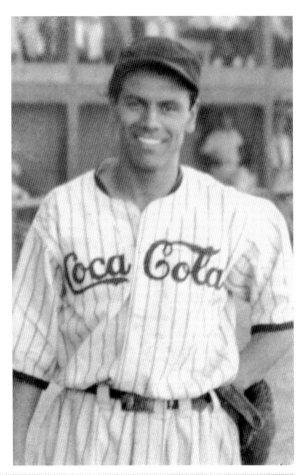

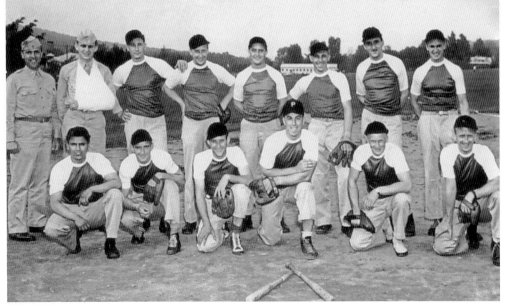

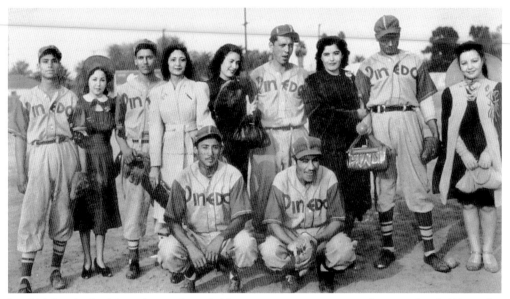

In 1936, Joe Andrade's pitching talents led him to win a game against the great Satchel Paige; he also hit a double off of Paige. Perhaps more impressive was when Andrade beat the top-ranked San Diego Hoover High School team during a 1930s tournament. He pitched a three-hitter against Hoover and struck out future Hall of Famer Ted Williams. Joe's talent was undeniable; however, his nationality and dark skin complexion did not allow him to pursue baseball at the professional level. Above, he is with the 1941 Celaya, Guanajuato, team (second row, third from left). Below, he (second row, second from right) poses with the 1939 Baja, California, Nacionales team. Andrade received a scholarship from USC, but he could not accept it because his family's financial situation required that he stay in Calexico and help contribute. A street is named after Andrade near Calexico High School. (Courtesy of Rosemary Andrade and Steve Binder.)

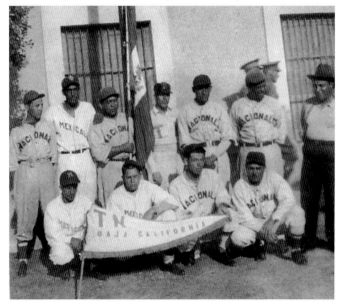

INLAND EMPIRE

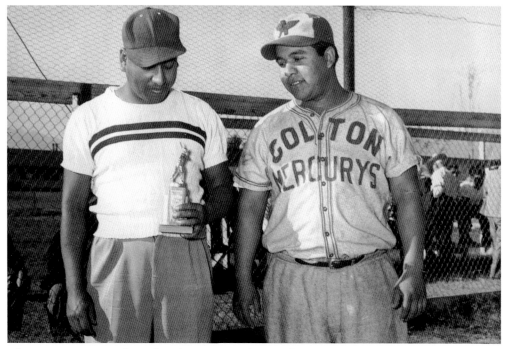

Chevo Martínez was a legendary figure in Southern California baseball history. He managed the Mitla Café championship teams of the late 1940s and went on to manage the Colton Mercuries (sometimes spelled Mercurys) to various championship titles as well. Martínez was known as a passionate manager who was not afraid to be vocal. He, like many others who lived in San Bernardino and Colton, worked for the Santa Fe Railroad for the majority of his life. But, weekends were dedicated to baseball games. Many people who knew Martínez have stated that if there were not racial restrictions in professional baseball, he could have been an excellent major-league manager. In the above photograph, Martínez (left) and Teo Duarte hold their trophy for winning the Orange Belt Baseball League in 1951. Below, he (left) accepts a trophy for managing the Colton Mercuries to another championship title.

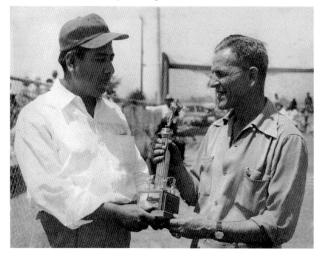

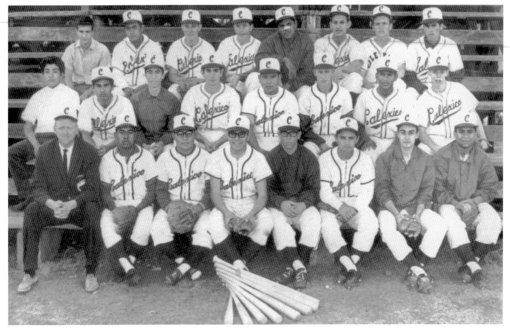

The 1964 Calexico Bulldogs finished in second place in the Imperial Valley League. The Brawley Wildcats were the dominant team, sending players like Sid Monge, Rudy Seánez, and Sergio Romo to the major leagues. The Bulldogs included John King, Mike Welisch, Mike Navarro, George Sierra, Jesus Amarillas, George Cisneros, Larry Iten, David Acuña, Fred Yturralde, Alex Armenta, Guy Yturralde, and Conrado Leyvas. Over 90 percent of this team received college degrees. Victor Wilson is in the third row, far left. (Courtesy of Victor Wilson.)

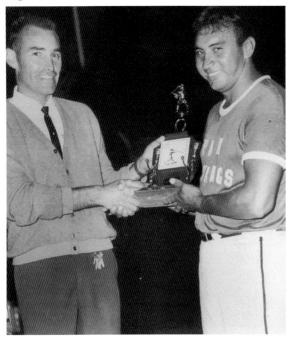

Don Allen, the Riverside recreation supervisor (left), presents Victor Reyes of Palm Springs's Mexican Colony with a runner-up trophy. Reyes was a four-year varsity letterman in baseball at Palm Springs High School in the early 1950s. He received the Alan Hall award for Palm Springs High School athlete of the year in 1956. Reyes's decorated baseball career was punctuated when he won the 1958 batting title in the Springs Desert Softball League.

INLAND EMPIRE

The Abril twins served in the Korean War. Ernie (right) and Manuel (left) escorted Marilyn Monroe during her visit to entertain the troops. They were part of the Army's Golden Dragons. The brothers escorted high-ranking officers, including generals, on the battlefield. *Los cuates* (the twins), born and raised in south Colton, were star players for the famous Colton Mercuries teams. They played in Mexico during the winter months, where they socialized with Pedro Infante. (Courtesy of Ray Rodríguez.)

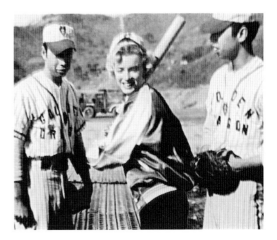

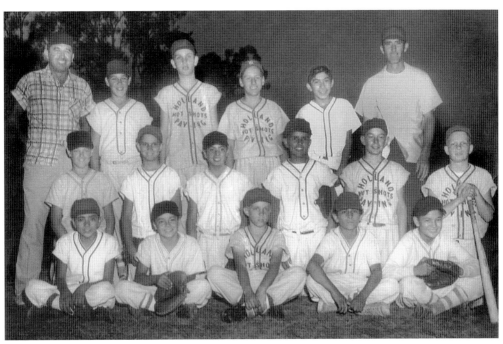

Rey Leon (first row, far left), born in Pomona and raised in Upland, picked lemons during the summers. He played for the 1957 Upland Little League team. Leon later played Pony League and varsity baseball. One of his teammate was Rollie Fingers, who had a distinguished major-league career. Rey's two brothers and cousin played baseball and softball. One of his brothers, Sam, played softball in the military. In the 1970s, Leon played for the Mid-Valley Brewers, a Mexican American team. (Courtesy of Rey Leon.)

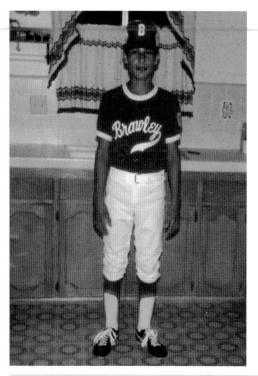

Rudy Seánez, born in Brawley, was drafted by the Cleveland Indians and later played for the Dodgers. Seánez's best season came in 2005, when he set career highs in wins and games pitched and posted a 2.69 ERA. He owns Seánez Sports Academy, which provides recreational opportunities for young men and women. Rudy and his wife, Dianna, keep their community close to their hearts by providing gifts and donations to students. (Courtesy of Rudy Seánez.)

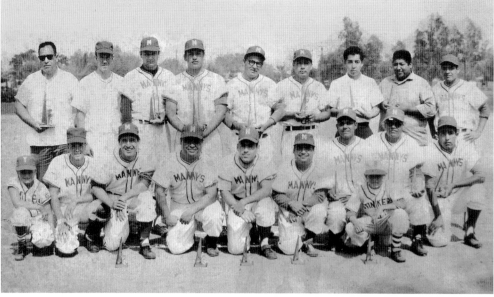

Manny's baseball team from San Bernardino won several Sunset League titles during the 1960s. The team's sponsor, Manny Chávez, is in the second row, far left, wearing his trademark shades. When the team won games, Chávez often treated players to drinks at his bar, located on Mount Vernon Avenue. Notable players on various Manny's teams included Joe Acosta, Chris Laguna, Manuel Martínez, Joe Ortiz, Pete Carrasco, Danny Carrasco, Robert Carrasco Jr. (manager), Felix Gómez, Alex Rubalcava, Jess Acosta, Pete Mata, and Ysidro Suárez.

7

COAST TO COAST

By the first two decades of the 20th century, Mexican communities could be found in nearly every state in the nation in large urban centers, small towns, and rural areas. Their remarkable and visionary leaders, despite overt discrimination, had established the solid foundation that eventually provided permanency and a secure social environment for subsequent generations of Mexican Americans. Their principal strategy, dating to 1848, was to create an infrastructure of organizations deeply rooted in mutual self-reliance and political empowerment. The Mexican leadership was absolutely vigilant about protecting its community interests and securing a firm family life. This community sovereignty and multiplicity of needs were evident in the essential development of mutual-aid societies, art galleries, businesses, religious associations, youth groups, music and theatre ensembles, women's clubs, Spanish-language newspapers, civil and labor alliances, political interest groups, human services, and sports leagues.

They reflected a broad diversity of political philosophies, social and economic classes, regional traditions, linguistic variations, religious thought, occupations, housing discrepancies, degrees of cultural assimilation, and gender. Regardless of their complex differences, the Mexican community established an elaborate network of sports activities as a form of social entertainment, solidarity, political empowerment, and cultural affirmation. Baseball, softball, basketball, football, soccer, and boxing were key elements within the community, providing a temporary distraction from a hostile environment.

The most popular sport was baseball and, later, softball. There were different types of teams. Companies sponsored industrial baseball teams, often dominated by Mexican players. In addition, Mexican businesses supported teams generally known as the Merchants. Neighborhood teams were also very prominent and popularly known as the "AC's," (Athletic Club). Many communities sponsored an adolescent team, the Juvenil Club. Mutual-aid societies supported teams, as did the Catholic Church, whose teams were often referred to as the "Guadalupanas." Besides male teams, many communities formed women's softball teams. In the post–World War II period, groups such as the Woodmen of the World (Los Hacheros del Mundo), the American GI Forum, and the League of United Latin American Citizens (LULAC) promoted their own teams. No matter where Mexicans settled throughout the United States, Sunday afternoons were dedicated to baseball.

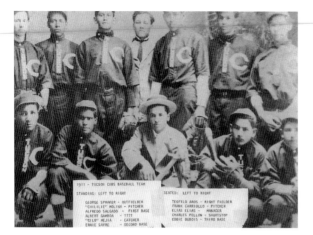

1911 - TUCSON CUBS BASEBALL TEAM

STANDING: LEFT TO RIGHT

GEORGE SPRAKER - OUTFIELDER
"CHILLIE" MOLINA - PITCHER
ALFREDO SALGADO - FIRST BASE
ALBERT SAMBOA - ????
"GILO" MEJIA - CATCHER
ERNIE SAYRE - SECOND BASE

SEATED: LEFT TO RIGHT

TEOFILO AROS - RIGHT FIELDER
FRANK CARRIOLLO - PITCHER
ELIAS ELIAS - MANAGER
CHARLES PELLON - SHORTSTOP
EDDIE DUBOIS - THIRD BASE

Charles Mancera Pellón (first row, second from right) was born in 1897 in Tucson, Arizona. He worked as a boilermaker apprentice for the Southern Pacific Railroad. In 1915, Pellón was a National Guard soldier patrolling the US side of the Mexican border during Pancho Villa's revolt. Pellón was stationed with the Infantry Division in France during World War I. (Courtesy of Darcy Quinlan Meyer).

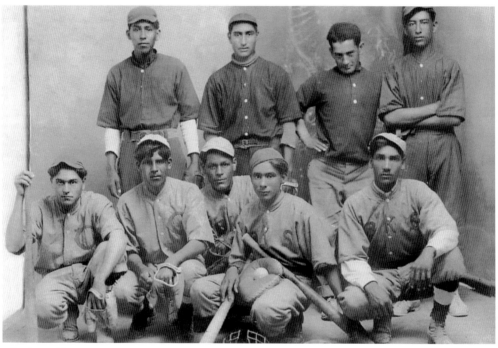

Charlie Pellón's mischievous pose sans cap provides a glimpse into his personality. True to his pedigree—his parents were actors/entertainers—he loved to clown around. His father was also a local civic leader and a founding member of the Alianza Hispano Americana, a civil and political-rights organization. Charlie returned to work at the Southern Pacific Railroad, and in 1922 he married Sarah Quiroz Romero. The couple had four daughters. Charlie's civic duties included being a founding member of the Benefits Sports Club. (Courtesy of Darcy Quinlan Meyer.)

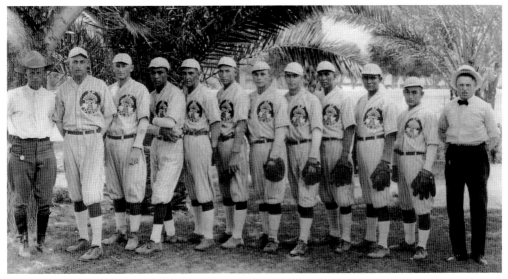

After 21 years with Southern Pacific, Charlie (second from right) drove a Tucson city garbage truck and then became a custodian at his alma mater elementary school. His third daughter, Grace, loved baseball and became his sidekick. She played competitive softball in Tucson and California for nearly 40 years and still found time to raise seven children. She is now 82 years old. So far, nearly half of Charlie and Sarah's 89 descendants have a baseball or softball background. (Courtesy of Darcy Quinlan Meyer.)

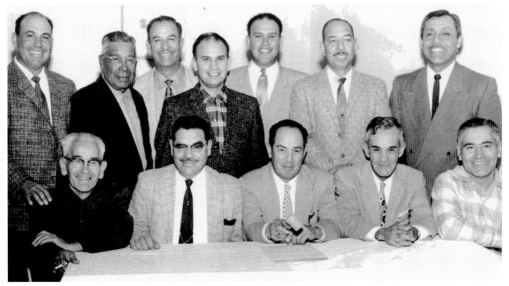

The Benefit Sports Club, a 40-60 team, was formed in 1965 and continued until 1998. The group was established to boost sports in the old pueblo of Tucson. The club was supported by admissions taken at their games. They raised money to buy uniforms and balls for a city recreational team. The officers were Fred Moreno, Gilbert Carrillo, Pete Pellón, Marcus Ronquillo, Gil Bravo, Aggie Aguilar, Louis Gutiérrez, Charles Pellón, Floretino Arcinega, Al Mills, Art Ortiz, and Joe Valenzuela. (Courtesy of Darcy Quinlan Meyer.)

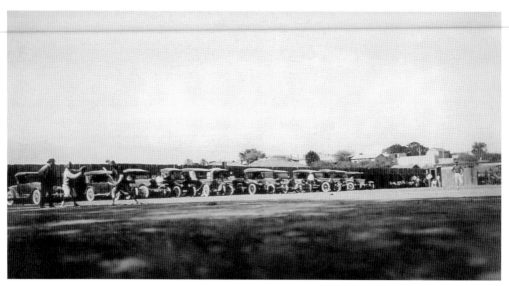

The 1912 Tucson Groves played their games at Elysian Grove Field, when Sundays meant barrio baseball. Manuel Padilla was recruited from Tucson High School as an all-league catcher. Elysian Grove Field had limited seating, so fans watched the games from cars outside the foul lines; this made for excellent viewing. Elysian Grove is presently the site of Ochoa Elementary School. Manuel Padilla's son Al later became an outstanding player and coach in Los Angeles. (Courtesy of Al Padilla.)

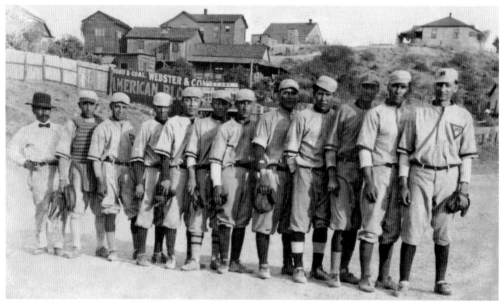

During the 1920s, copper mines were prevalent throughout Arizona. Due to the political climate of the time, the only jobs available to Mexicans were menial and low paying. Baseball, a popular sport in Mexico, was one of the many community activities people enjoyed, with teams traveling from town to town. Pictured here is a team from the Globe-Miami area. Luz Ramos, a pitcher, is fourth from the right, and his brother Tomas, a catcher, is second from left. (Courtesy of Tim Ramos.)

COAST TO COAST

Leonard Calderón, owner of Calderón Ballroom, was public minded and involved in many community activities. This is the local Mexican American baseball team he sponsored. On the far left is Leonard's son Nano. In the back row, second from the right, is Junior Verdugo, one of the owners of Oaxaca's Mexican Restaurant in downtown Phoenix. (Courtesy of the Calderón family.)

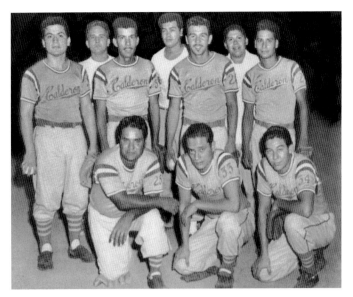

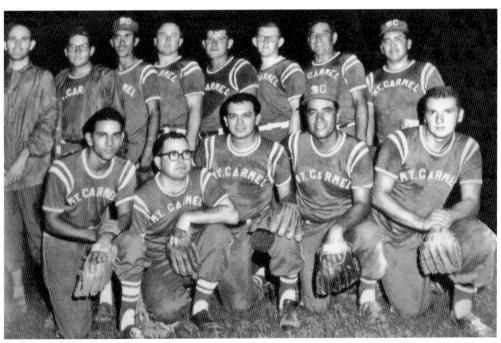

Our Lady of Mount Carmel (OLMC) baseball team participated in the Mesa League in Tempe, Arizona, around 1959. The OLMC team created unity by representing Mount Carmel Parish in the baseball league. The only player identified in this photograph is Cano Pérez (second row, far right).

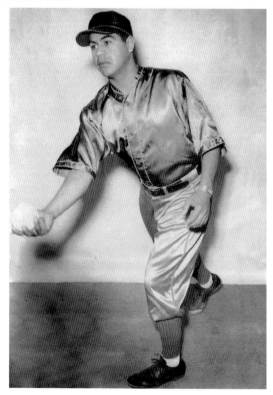

After graduating from Anaheim High School in 1937, Ray Ortez immediately headed off to Prescott, Arizona, to play fast-pitch softball for the Prescott Tavern team. Ortez was recruited as the no.-1 hurler for the team. He was in the thick of things, right from the start, going up against seasoned veteran Nolly Trujillo of the Tom's Tavern team from Phoenix. Ortez beat Trujillo for his first victory. In the 1938 softball season, Ortez was recruited by Tom's Tavern, becoming Trujillo's teammate. (Courtesy of Monica Ortez.)

Ray Ortez was picked up by the Phoenix Lettuce Kings in 1938, which won the Arizona State Softball and American Softball Association national championships. Ortez hurled the team to victory in the final game of the championship series. In the bottom of the eighth inning, Ortez asked all of his defensive teammates to stand behind him, except the catcher and two fielders. He then threw perfect pitches over home plate, striking out the side while his team played cards behind the mound. (Courtesy of Monica Ortez.)

COAST TO COAST

Ray Ortez and his new bride, Florence Spencer, headed to Salt Lake City, Utah, barely making the opening of the 1939 spring softball season with the Exchange Club. Ortez, the no.-1 pitcher for the team, did so magnificently during the season that the Exchange Club won the 1939 Utah state championship. The Exchange Club finished in third place at the national tournament. During the season, Ortez became a father with his first daughter, Marlita Ann. (Courtesy of Monica Ortez.)

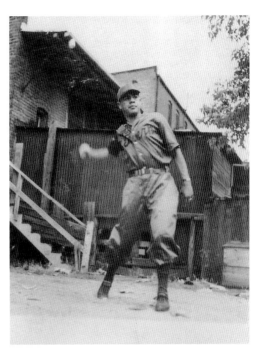

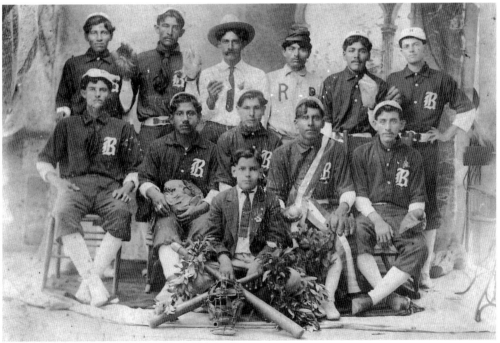

The only person identified on this 1909 Rockport, Texas, team is Joe F. Garza (the young boy in front). Joe was the brother of Ben Garza, founder of the LULAC. Joe moved to Corpus Christi after returning from World War I and was active in the American Legion in the 1920s. He later became active in politics, equal education for Mexican children, and sports. (Dr. Héctor P. García Papers, Texas A&M University–Corpus Christi.)

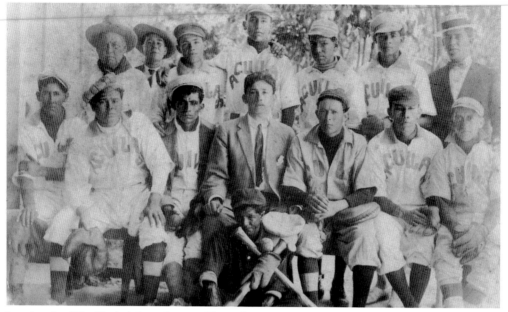

Las Aguilas (The Eagles) from Corpus Christi became a popular team in the 1900s, playing other Mexican American teams in the city and from other towns. A favorite event was when Las Aguilas played each other, pitting *los gordos* (the fat ones) against *los flacos* (the skinny ones). The game brought laughter and shouts from spectators. The only player identified in this 1929 image is Ralph Galvan Sr. (first row, far left). (Vernon Smylie Papers, Texas A&M University–Corpus Christi.)

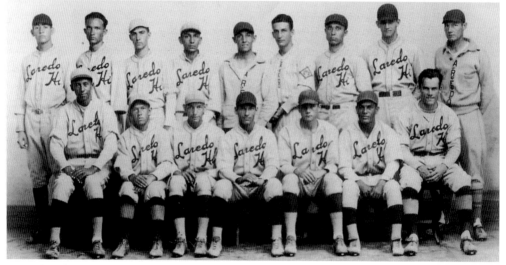

More than half of the Laredo Tigers' innings in 1926 were pitched by Johnny Dickinson Gutiérrez. He attended Texas A&M and later was a CPA in Laredo and Mexico. Shown here are, from left to right, (first row) Fernando Cordero, L. Salazar, Albert Esparza, Rogelio García, Gary Burr, Pablo Escamilla, and Leon Fortaissain; (second row) Johnny Dickinson, George Crabb, ? Rodríguez, Eloy Barrera, Kiki Mejia, Tom Leyendecker, Ellis Crabb, Tony Leyendecker, and coach Shirley DaCamara. (Courtesy of John Y. Dickinson III.)

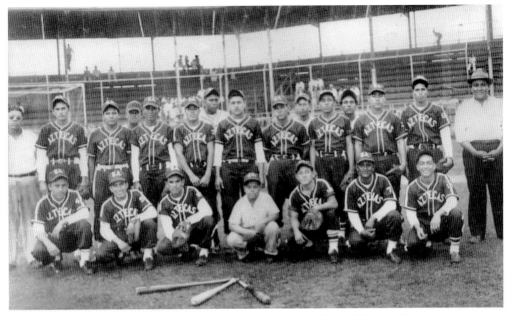

The Bryan, Texas, Aztecas was one of several teams established by the Mexican American community since the 1940s. Several players have come out of Bryan and nearby College Station. One of the first was Homer Thomas Martínez, who was a three-year letterman with the Aggies baseball team. Manuel García graduated from Consolidated High School in 1956 and lettered in baseball for four years; he was voted Most Valuable Player. Manuel returned to his former high school as the head baseball coach. (Courtesy of Lionel García.)

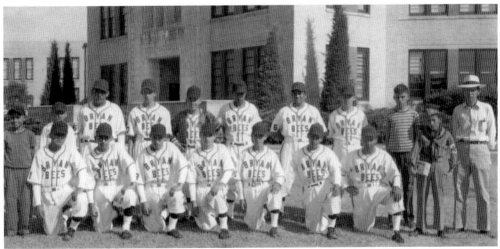

The Bryan Bees gather for a team photograph. The players are, from left to right, (first row) Nick Moncivias, Paul Rodríguez, Eusebio Gongara, Nino Gongara, Lalo Rocha, Manuel Rúiz, and Bonnie Martínez; (second row) batboys Vincent Rosas and Rudy Letterman, Armando Macías, Roy Marín, Martín Muñoz, Paul García, Steve Martínez, Richard Rodríguez, batboys Fred Rodríguez and Robert Canáles, and coach-manager is Pete Rodríguez. Pete worked at Texas A&M University for 52 years and served during World War II. (Courtesy of Lionel García.)

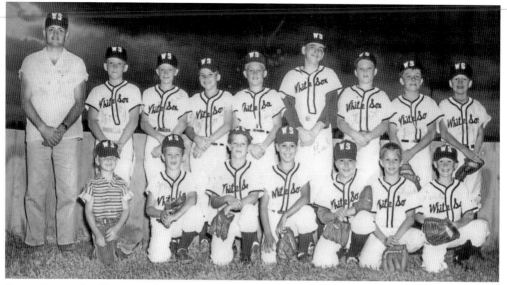

Sonny Benavidez (first row, third from right) played for the College Station, Texas, White Sox Little League team in 1957. Paul W. Bryant (second row, third from right) is the son of legendary football coach Paul "Bear" Bryant. Benavidez played four years of baseball at Consolidated High School (1960–1964). His father, Eusebio, moved the family to College Station in the 1940s. Mexican Americans worked at the Texas A&M mess hall and dorms. People enjoyed watching the Bees, Aztecas, and LULAC teams. (Courtesy of Sonny Benavidez.)

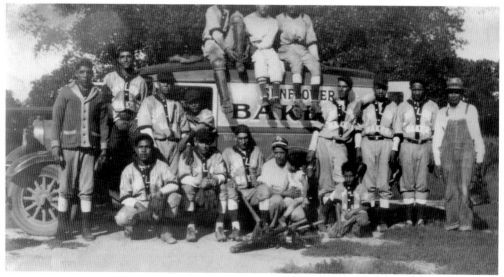

Kansas was a hotbed of countless Mexican American teams and leagues during the 1920s and 1930s. Teams could be found in Coffyville, Pittsburgh, Deerfield, Florence, Peabody, Syracuse, Parsons, Atchinson, Iola, Fredonia, and Harrington. This 1931 photograph is of the Topeka Sunflower Bakers. Some of the players include Perfecto Torres, Eladio Tostado, John González, Julián López, Chonilla Rocha, John Gomes, Tom Gomes, Jesús Del Hierro, Felipe Gomes, Tito Gomes, Lupe Cabrera, Nick Ochoa, and Baldomero Llames. (Courtesy of Hazel Gomez.)

Jay Martínez of Copeland, Kansas, was the catcher for the Dodge City Cowboys in 1947. Jay and his brother Ray helped lead another team to success, the Liberal, Kansas, Ban Johnson Blacksox. The Blacksox won the championship of the Western Division of the Ban Johnson League in the team's first year. The Western Division consisted of teams from other Kansas cities, including Dodge City, Garden City, Lerned, and Pratt. (Courtesy of Rod Martínez.)

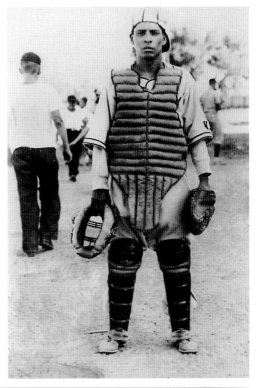

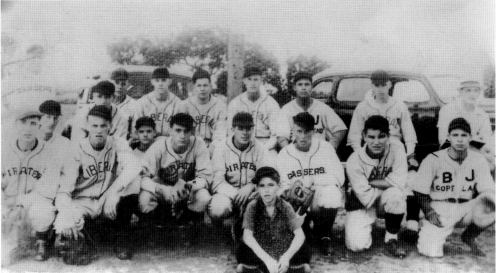

Members of the Liberal, Kansas, Blacksox in 1939 included the Martínez brothers, Ray (second row, third from right) and Jay (first row, far right). Ray and Jay were born in Copeland, Kansas, of immigrant parents; they were the only Mexican American family in Copeland. The brothers were outstanding athletes in high school as four-year lettermen in football, basketball, and baseball. Ray played baseball in the Army Air Corps while stationed in England from 1944 to 1945, attached to a fighter squadron. (Courtesy of Rod Martínez.)

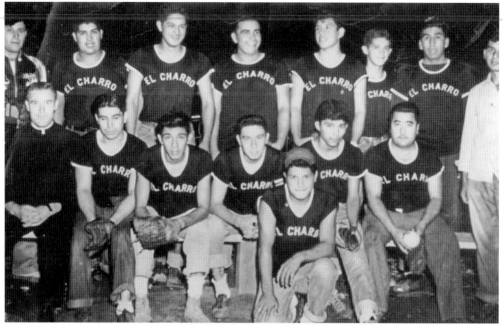

After World War II, softball became popular within Mexican American communities. In addition to games, annual tournaments were sponsored in several states, bringing together teams, families, and fans from several communities. Los Charros of Chanute, Kansas, were sponsored by St. Patrick's Catholic Church. The team, seen here in 1951, participated in the Chanute Softball Tournament from 1963 to 1979, attracting other teams from Kansas City, Topeka, Lawrence, Emporia, Newton, Wichita, Parsons, Hutchinson, and Salina. (Courtesy of John and Antonia Alonzo.)

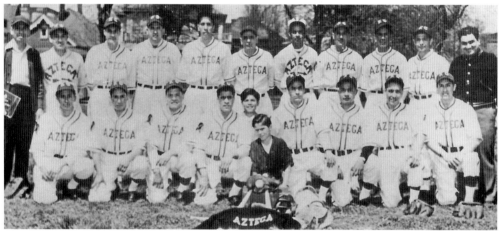

Joseph Morales Sr. (second row, fifth from left) played with the Kansas City, Kansas, Aztecas. He started playing for the Columbia Steel Company. After serving in the war, he began playing softball in 1946 and pitched and played center field for the Aztecas and later for the Stateline Locos. He stopped playing at the age of 55. He managed the Eagles, sponsored by American Legion Post No. 213. His son Joseph Jr. and grandsons Luke, Tony Jr., Greg, and Ben played for the Locos. (Courtesy of Catherine Morales.)

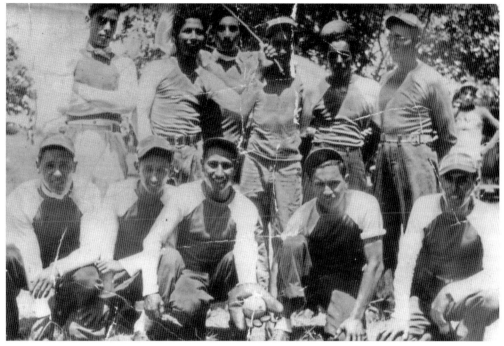

This 1946 Newton, Kansas, team was called the Mexican Catholics. Shown here are, from left to right, (first row) Frank Lujano, John Florez, Bill Lujano, Maggie Gómez, and Raymond Pedrosa; (second row) Bacho Rodríguez, unidentified, Ángel Rodríguez, unidentified, Frank Rodríguez, and Frank Florez. Several pairs of brothers and cousins often played on the same teams. A hat or basket was passed around to collect money for gas, food, and housing for the visiting teams. (Courtesy of Ray Oláis.)

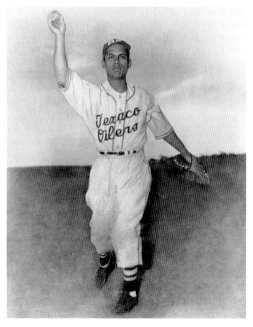

Ray Martínez was a member of the 1939 Woodward Oklahoma Oilers. A promising baseball career came his way when he was approached by Brooklyn Dodgers scout Bert Wells, who offered Martínez a professional contract of $90 a month plus housing and food. Martínez turned down the offer because he was making more money playing for the Liberal, Kansas, Blacksox. These teams paid their players decent salaries and provided good jobs, preventing them from being taken by professional teams. (Courtesy of Rod Martínez.)

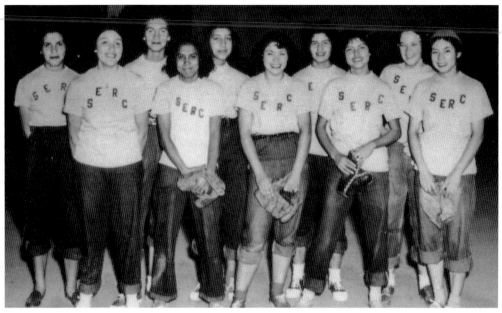

Washington Grade School had been attended by Mexican students. The building was donated to Our Lady of Guadalupe Church, which renamed it the South East Recreation Center. The Scottsbluff girls' softball team was sponsored by the center during the 1940s and 1950s. The players shown here are, from left to right, (first row) Nadine García, Ramona Olmos, Martha Medina, Sara Miramontez, and Vicki Pérez; (second row) Mary Ann Dorador, Virginia Macias, Virginia Domínguez, Amelia Dorador, and Jenny Pérez.

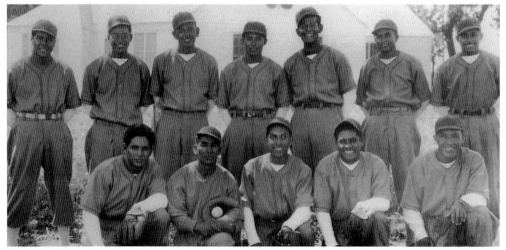

This 1946 Bayard Tigers team played in the Mission League in western Nebraska. Nearly all the towns had a Catholic mission church attended by farmworker families. Thus, the baseball teams played in the Mission League. Teams included Scottsbluff, Mitchell, Lyman, Morrill, Bayard, Gering, Minatare, Alliance, and Torrington, Wyoming. Shown here are, from left to right, (first row) Enrique Vera, Tomas Moreno, Federico Chávez, Leocadio Vera, and Basilio Gonzáles; (second row) Ernesto Plaza, Luis Gonzáles, Isidro Flores, Juan Negrete, Francisco Flores Jr., Albert Abeyta, and Wally Vera.

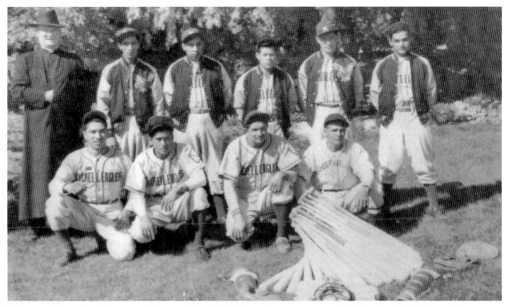

Players whose families were farmworkers had their housing provided by the GW Sugar Company. This is the first Eagles team from Mitchell in 1946. Shown here are, from left to right, (first row) Joe Vega, Conrad Huerta, Senovio Reyes, and Bart Zapata; (second row) Fr. Patrick Moriety, Daniel Muro, Paul Núñez, Mariano Fonseca, Camelo Reyes, and Jerry Marín. Other ex-Eagles included Phillip Vargas, Jesse Lara, Tony Márquez, Rudy Garza, Benjamín Muro, Harry Guzmán, Tony Carrasco, Bob Garza, Salvador Huerta, Louie Narváiz, and David Rodríguez.

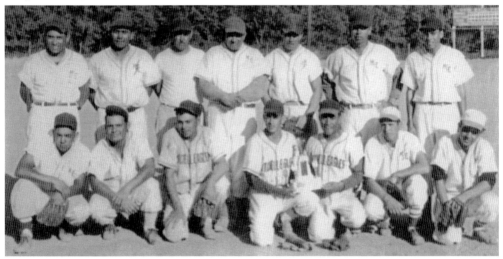

Financial support for families was farm-related manual labor and railroad work. Some men worked in a meatpacking plant, and a few were employed in downtown businesses. They practiced baseball after work. This 1955 Mitchell Eagles team is shown in Julesburg, Colorado. Posing are, from left to right, (first row) Ralph Miranda, Louie Velásquez, Ralph Castañeda, Phillip Huerta, Sam Razo, Isabel Ramírez, and Harvey Ventura; (second row) manager Conrad Huerta, Eddy Guzmán, Paul Girón, Senovio Reyes, Camelo Reyes, Marshall Reyes, and Pasqual Huerta Jr.

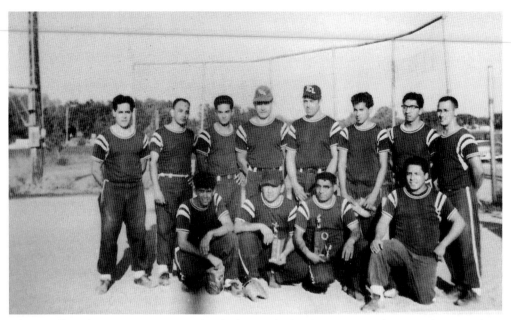

Almost all students at some point checked out of school to start working in the sugar beet fields; few students attended school beyond the sixth grade. The 1950s Third City Latins played ball in Grand Island in east-central Nebraska. Baseball was a popular means of recreation and entertainment. Shown here are, from left to right, (first row) Jesse Galván, Mario Ramírez, Sunny Aguilar (manager), and Seraphine Aguilar; (second row) Philip Salinas, Pete Sánchez, Gilbert Mora, Robert Briseño, Ignacio Valdez, unidentified, Manuel Aguilar, and Katerino Salinas.

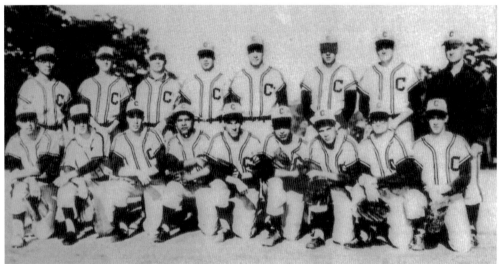

The 1964 Chadron State College team included Mauricio Martín Ramírez (first row, fourth from left). He received his BA degree from Chadron and his MA and PhD from the University of Nebraska at Lincoln. He has received the Nebraska Hispanic Man of the Year award and the National Hispanic Man of the Year award by the LULAC in Corpus Christi, Texas. He served in Vietnam in 1968–1969 and is the recipient of the Purple Heart.

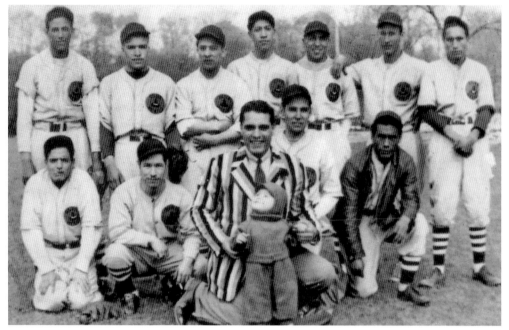

In the summer of 1940, Boric's Club Mexico sponsored a baseball team in Milwaukee's municipal Double-A League. In its inaugural season, George Robles hit over .300, and the team's star pitcher, Tony Cuellar, pitched a no-hitter. Unfortunately, Cuellar broke his leg sliding into second base in the very next game. The team finished the season in fourth place. With America's involvement in World War II looming, the team disbanded in 1941.

Jovita Duran (first row, second from left) came to the West Side of Chicago from Texas. She played on this championship team in 1936, the Moreloettes, sponsored by the Methodist settlement Marcy House. The team name was a feminine version of Morelos, a team from the same area. Duran's husband of 64 years, Frank Duran, was a catcher for the Morelos. South Side girls' teams like the Moreloettes and the Amapolas traveled all around Chicago to play. (Courtesy of Mexican Chicago.)

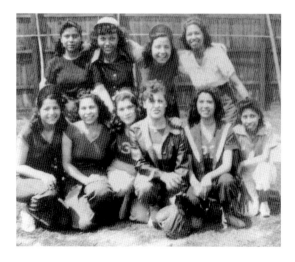

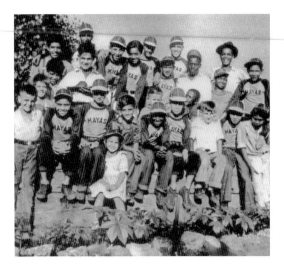

Young people pose in the Mexican American community of South Chicago, Illinois, in the 1930s. Like countless Mexican neighborhoods in the United States, the South Chicago community named its teams after the great indigenous groups from Mexico, including the Aztecas, the Mayans, and the Yaquis. Parents encouraged children to play sports in order to learn social skills and to keep from getting into trouble with gangs and alcohol and to avoid run-ins with the police. (Courtesy of the Southeast Chicago Project.)

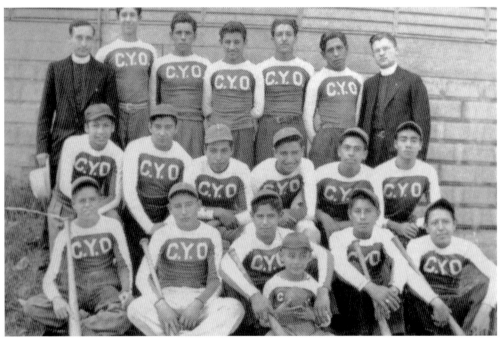

The Catholic Church sponsored Mexican American teams, including this 1930s Catholic Youth Organization team in East Chicago, Indiana. The church hierarchy, unsure how to treat Mexican immigrants arriving in their communities, established segregated churches for them. Players on this team included Dominic Cruz, Robert Segovia, Albert Mancera, Frank Vásquez, Fernand Mirelis, Louis Vásquez, Louis Martines, Tony Leyba, Raymond Vega, Fernando Leyba, Santos Godoy, Tony Verial, and Marselo Moreno. A few players still reside in East Chicago. (Courtesy of Señoras of Yesteryear.)

8

FIELD OF DREAMS

Since its inception in 2006, the Latino Baseball History Project has been enthusiastically engaged in several activities, including its Mexican American baseball pictorial book series, library exhibits, newsletters, player reunions, oral interviews, and first-pitch ceremonies. The main mission of these activities is to preserve and promote the long and rich history of Mexican American baseball and softball within the American sports narrative. For many surviving ballplayers, this long overdue acknowledgment, in the ninth inning of their lives, has instilled in them an awareness that their noteworthy contributions are now being publicly recognized and chronicled.

Family members have observed that this unlooked-for attention has renewed the physical and cerebral lives of these players, who have become, once again, heroes and celebrities in their families, neighborhoods, and the larger community. These players have generously contributed vintage photographs, invaluable stories, and irreplaceable uniforms and equipment to the Latino Baseball History Project. In interviews, players have unselfishly expressed gratitude to their loved ones and shared how much their families supported them and sacrificed during their playing days. Moreover, these players have served as powerful role models, as subsequent generations followed in their illustrious footsteps in playing the national pastime. It is not unusual to discover families with four generations of players due to the sway of their baseball elders.

This generational inspiration especially rings true with the widespread influence that female ballplayers had on their daughters, granddaughters, great-granddaughters, and nieces. Sadly, countless players have gone to the big ballpark in the sky without knowing that their immense skills on the field would someday be publicly validated. Numerous families of deceased ballplayers have been a big part of the project, insuring that the legacy of these extraordinary players will be archived.

In this and each of the previous three books in the series on Mexican American baseball, a chapter is included entitled "Field of Dreams," which presents current information about surviving ballplayers and/or their families. This chapter distinctly pays tribute to these extended families, especially the contemporary players who continue to honor the spirit of their ancestors by sitting in the dugout, standing inside the batter's box, running the base paths, throwing from the mound, and roaming in the outfield. Play ball!

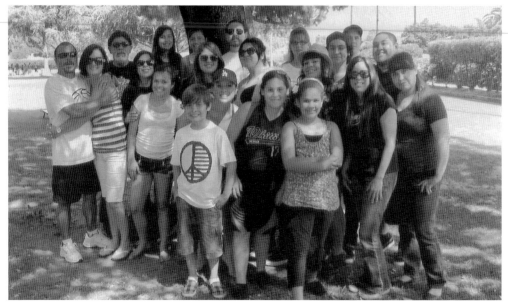

Tony Armenta's descendants gather in 2013 for a game at Michigan Park in Whittier, California. Armenta, a pitcher, played throughout the 1940s in Los Angeles along with his brothers Paul, Joe, Oscar, and Ray, who served as his catcher. Tony's son Chuck (third from left) played with his uncle Ray. Grandson Chuck Armenta Jr. (far left) coached the Jurupa Valley High School team. In 2010, he was named the High School GameTime Baseball Coach of the Year. (Courtesy of Bea Armenta Dever.)

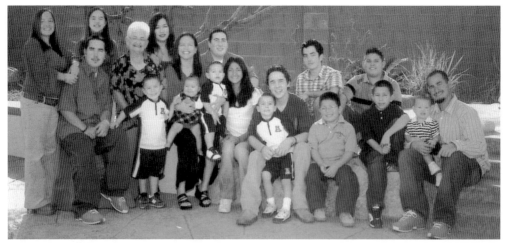

Grace Pellón Quinlan poses with her grandchildren and great-grandchildren in 2006. Since that time, nine more great-grandchildren have been born. Grace's father was an outstanding baseball player in Arizona in the first two decades of the 20th century. Grace herself played for 40 years. Of her seven children, six played ball. All 11 grandchildren played Little League, and some played in high school and in other leagues. Grace has had seven great-grandsons that played or are playing Little League and one great-granddaughter playing Little League softball. (Courtesy of Darcy Quinlan Meyer.)

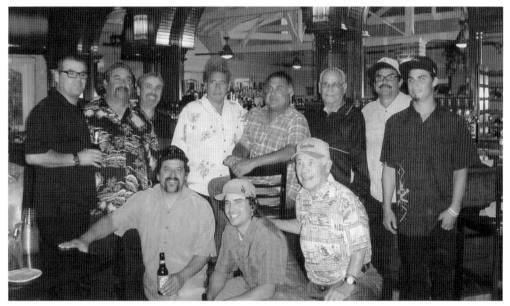

Mexican Americans from Catalina Island played high school ball, establishing winning records. After all, they practiced and played in a major-league park, Wrigley Field, where the Cubs held spring training on the island. This photograph was taken in April 2013. Shown here are, from left to right, (first row) Joe Hernández Sr., Joe Hernández Jr., and Marcelino Saucedo; (second row) Raúl Hernández, Richard Hernández, Don McLeish, Gil Voci, Jo Jo Machado, Joe Saucedo, Gil Hernández Sr., and Gil Hernández Jr. (Courtesy of Marcelino Saucedo.)

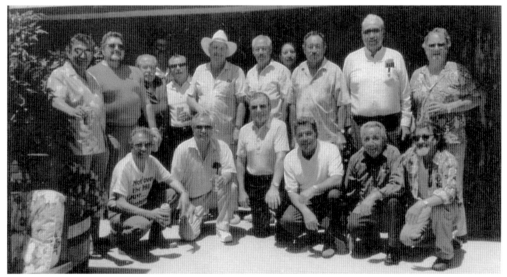

The Burbank Boys played baseball and softball at all competitive levels and often hosted neighborhood reunions, including this one in the early 1970s. Gathered here are, from left to right, (first row) Art Lara, Sal Moreno, Frank Noriega, Albert Ruiz, Robert Télles, and Cirilo Gonzáles; (second row) Frank Roque, Ralph Gallegos, Fred Ballesteros, Ray Díaz, Alex Sáenz, Casey Vásquez, Joe Madrid, Conrad Rentería, Charlie García, and Albert Sáenz. (Courtesy of Joffee García.)

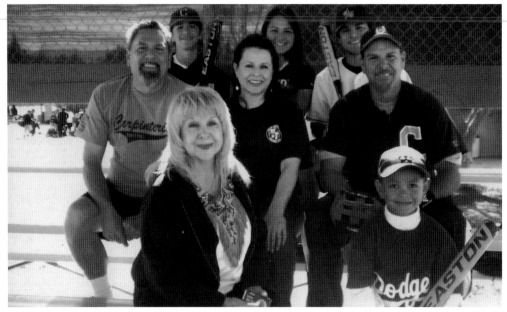

Four generations of Orozcos gather at the Northridge Little League Fields in Northridge, California, in a memorial to recently deceased Joseph Orozco. From left to right are (first row) Elisa Orozco and her great-nephew Timmy Orozco; (second row) Elisa's nephew Alonzo E. Orozco Jr., her daughter Rose-Mary Festich, and nephew Martin Orozco; (third row) Martin's children Roberto Clemente Orozco, Stephanie Orozco, and Martin Orozco Jr. Timmy is Martin's fourth child. (Courtesy of Al Orozco.)

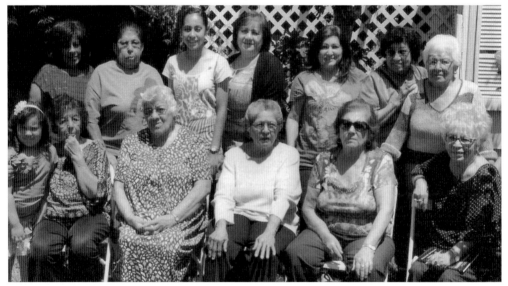

A book-signing event in the San Fernando Valley took place on April 28, 2013, at the home of Ramona Valenzuela. This group photograph represents four generations of female softball players. Shown here are, from left to right, (first row) Alexis García, Ramona Valenzuela, Conchita Delgado, Lucy Castillo, Stella Quijada, and Teresa Hernández; (second row) Yolanda García, Terry Hernández, Rachel Reyes, Licha Hernández, Rita Duarte, Isabelle Vaíz, and Nellie García.

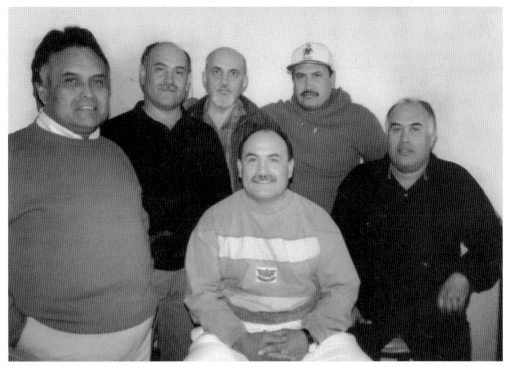

The Lizalde brothers were raised in Guadalupe, California. All of them played baseball at Santa Maria High School, and five of them played baseball or football at either Allan Hancock College, San Diego State University, Los Angeles City College, or Gonzaga University. They have devoted their entire lives to teaching and coaching. They are, from left to right, (first row) Fred, Lenny, and Herb; (second row) Milo, Manuel, and John. Among them, they have a master's degree, bachelor's degrees, and teaching credentials. (Courtesy of the Lizalde family.)

Cesarío Estrada, born in North Platte, Nebraska, joined the Army in 1949 and was wounded in the Korean War. He was awarded two Purple Hearts and three Bronze Stars. In 1970, he was sent to Vietnam, where he earned his fourth Bronze Star. Between wars, he was a drill sergeant at Fort Ord, California. He played baseball throughout Nebraska, Kansas, and Colorado with his brothers and cousins. He is holding a vintage photograph in which he is seen as a batboy. He resides in Modesto, California.

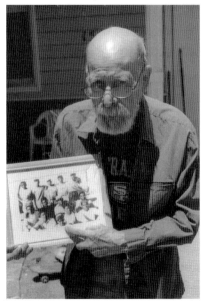

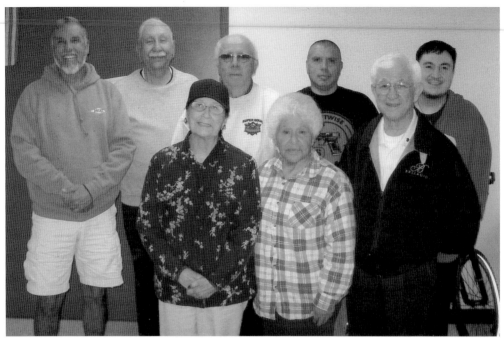

Generations of baseball and softball players shared their recollections at the Montebello Historical Society on February 7, 2013. The stories were very emotional for everyone in attendance because the speakers had several things in common: pride, passion, and love for the game. Pictured here are, from left to right, (first row) Consuelo Solis, Nora Morales, and Bob Lagunas; (second row) Phil Vásquez, Joseph Holguín, Armando Pérez, James Henninger Aguirre, and Davey Escobedo. (Courtesy of James Henninger Aguirre.)

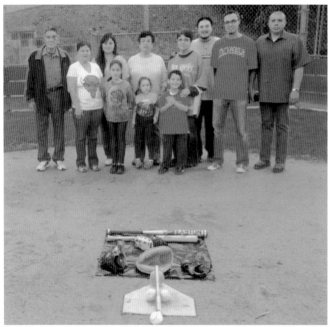

The Aguirre, Henninger, De La Ossa, Barry, Escobedo, Longoria, and Galván families have a long tradition of playing baseball and softball—dating back 100 years. The families are proud and honored to be part of the rich history of Mexican American baseball and softball and to be passing the grand old game to newer generations. They believe that regardless of race, color, or creed everyone should be given the opportunity to play. (Courtesy of James Henninger Aguirre.)

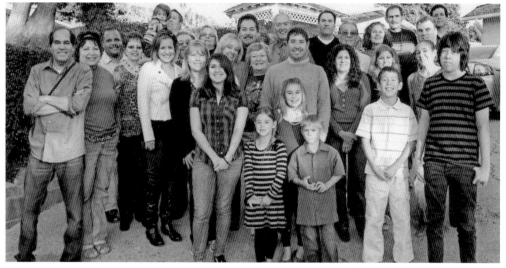

Rudy Regalado (back right, with sunglasses) garnered baseball honors at Glendale High School and played at USC as well as for the Cleveland Indians, which included a trip to the 1954 World Series. Sam Regalado (back row, center, with mustache) is a baseball historian and professor at California State University at Stanislaus. Ron Regalado (first row, far left) is an art director at the Walt Disney Company. Ron's father, Greg, was a key member of the Los Angeles 40-60 Baseball Club. (Courtesy of Ron Regalado.)

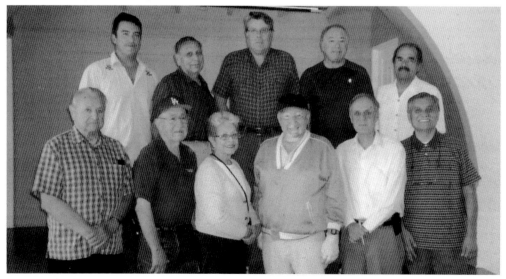

In 2012, the Carpinteria Mexican American community and the Curious Cup, owned by Kiona Gross, sponsored a book-signing event. Ed Arellano helped make the event successful. Prof. Jose Alamillo, from the California State University at Channel Islands, chaired the history panel, which included Jim Campos, Eddie Navarro, and Joe Talaugon. Participants include, from left to right, (first row) Ed Arellano, Dan Manríquez, Lucy Díaz, Reg Velásquez, Campos, and Richard Santillán; (second row) Dave Granada, Mario Robledo, Richard Sanchez, Rick Medel, and Fritz Velasquez. (Courtesy of Ed Arellano.)

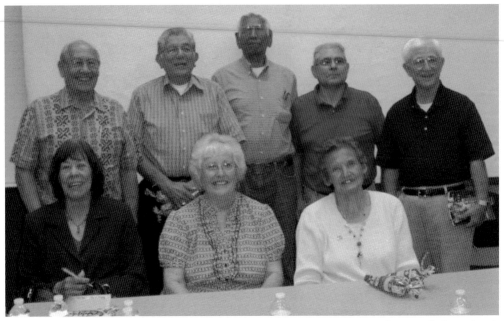

On April 27, 2013, a baseball event was held at Santa Ana Community College, including a book signing, a panel discussion, and a slide presentation. The hostess was Angelina F. Veyna, professor of Chicano studies and history. Poet Alejandro Moreno read a baseball poem, and players and their adult children shared wonderful stories. Gathered here are, from left to right, (first row) Rosie Gómez, Bea Dever, and Carmen Luna; (second row) Richard Méndez, Jim Segovia, José G. Felipe, Rod Martínez, and Bob Lagunas. (Courtesy of Susan C. Luévano.)

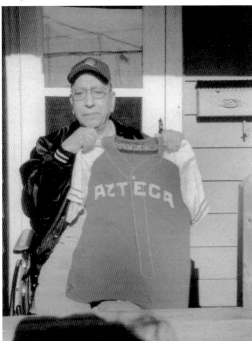

Joe Morales displays his original 1948 Kansas City, Kansas, Azteca jersey in front of his home in 2002. His house is located in the Armourdale community across from Shawnee Park. Morales pitched for the Aztecas and several other teams. His jersey was mounted in a frame and preserved by his grandson Tony Oropeza Jr. After World War II, softball became a popular form of recreation, especially for returning veterans and wartime defense workers. (Courtesy of Catherine Morales.)

FIELD OF DREAMS

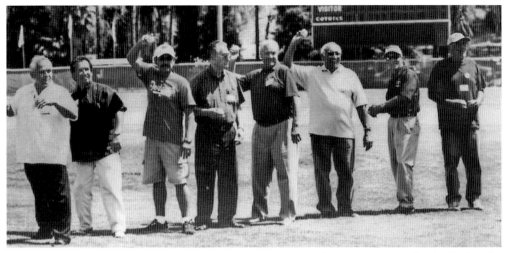

This 2012 first-pitch ceremony was held in San Bernardino between games of a double-header between California State University, San Bernardino and California State University at Dominguez Hills. From left to right are Al Villanueva, Ernie Benzor, Richard Cortéz, Carlos Uribe, Al Vásquez, Victor Reyes, Sal Valdivia, and Chico Briones. At these events, players select a family member to have the honor of catching their first pitch, and later families are invited onto the field for group photographs.

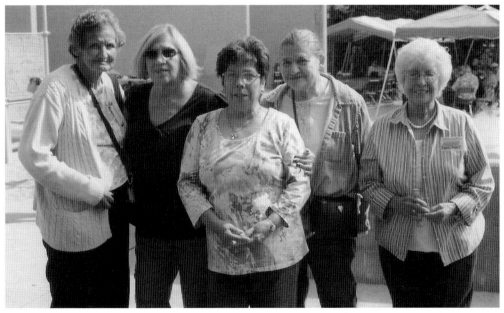

In 2012, the community of Logan in the city of Santa Ana, California, sponsored a reunion. Among the gathering were women who had played softball. From left to right are Carmen Luna Robles, Lupe Laguna Esparza, Theresa Ceja Flores, Sylvia Luna Oscequeda, and Mary Praga Moraga. Robles was one of the best players throughout Orange County. Moraga played in the 1930s. In her youth, Esparza dated Bill Medley of the famous Righteous Brothers, who wrote the song "Little Latin Lupe Lu" for her.

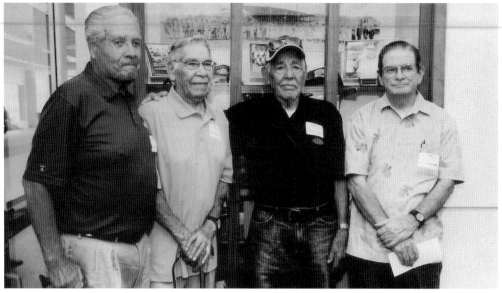

Each summer, the Latino Baseball History Project hosts a reunion that brings players and their families onto the campus of California State University, San Bernardino to celebrate the rich history of Mexican American baseball and softball. At the 2011 reunion, several outstanding players attended, including, from left to right, Al Vásquez, Tommie and Maury Encinas, and Alfonso Ledesma. In the background is an exhibit paying tribute to Mexican American baseball in the Inland Empire.

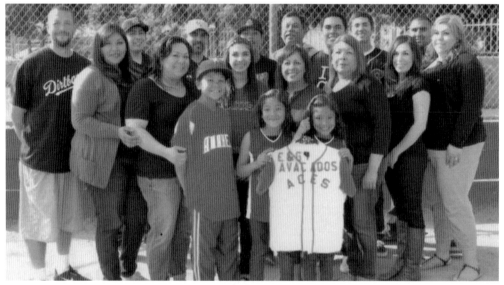

This late-1940s softball jersey was worn by Lolly Gómez Fuentes when she was 18 years old while playing for Los Aces from La Habra. Fuentes loved all sports, but she cherished softball with her best friend, Rosie. Lolly and her husband, John, saw their children, grandchildren, and great-grandchildren play baseball and softball. Lolly's family is seen in this photograph, including daughters Laura, Debra, Susan, and Stephanie; grandchildren Alex, Daniel, Joseph, Lisa, and Miguel; and great-grandchildren Victoria, Samantha, and Matthew; and son-in-law John Morales. (Courtesy of Patty Cardenas.)

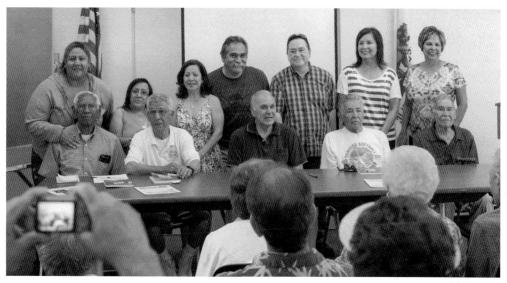

On June 8, 2013, a special event was held at the Pomona Public Library, which hosted a monthlong exhibit on Mexican American baseball and softball in the Pomona Valley. In addition, a panel of players and family members shared wonderful stories. The above photograph shows the sons, daughters, and a granddaughter with their fathers and grandfather. They are, from left to right, (first row) José Felipe, Gilbert Guevara, Bobby Duran, and Maury and Tommie Encinas; (second row) Mónica DeCasas Patterson, Mónica and Marie Guevara, Rudy and Richard Duran, Jernell Encinas Nieman, and Patti Encinas García. The players and sons of deceased players also took a group photograph before a book signing. In the photograph below are, from left to right, (first row) José Felipe, Gilbert Guevara, Bobby Duran, Maury and Tommie Encinas, and Peter Belmúdez; (second row) Richard Álvarez, Joey Fuentez, Al Vásquez, Buddy Muñoz, Al Guevara Jr., Al Villanueva Jr., Richard García, and Gilbert Belmúdez.

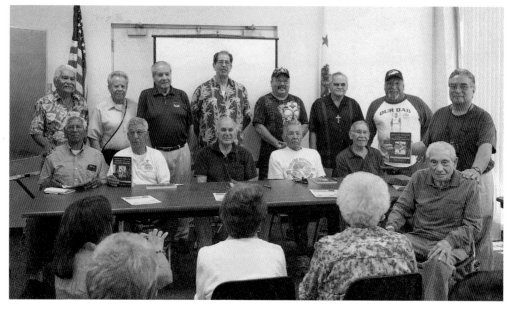

BIBLIOGRAPHY

Barajas, Frank P. *Curious Unions: Mexican American Workers and Resistance in Oxnard, California, 1898–1961*. Lincoln, NE: University of Nebraska Press, 2012.

Campos, Jim, et al. *Carpinteria*. Charleston, SC: Arcadia Publishing, 2007.

———, et al. *Greater Carpinteria, Summerland, and La Conchita*. Charleston, SC: Arcadia Publishing, 2009.

Docter, Christopher L. "The Great Awakening: A Comparative Analysis of Mexican American Baseball in the San Fernando Valley." Unpublished paper, 2012.

Gil, Carlos B. *We Became Mexican American: How Our Immigrant Family Survived to Pursue the American Dream*. Self-published, 2012.

Loomis, Derward. *San Fernando Retrospective: The First Fifty Years*. San Fernando: San Fernando Heritage, 1985.

Maulhardt, Jeffrey Wayne. *Oxnard: 1941–2004*. Charleston, SC: Arcadia Publishing, 2005.

———. *The Day the New York Giants Came to Oxnard*. Ventura, CA: Clark's Printing, 1997.

McCafferty, John D. *Aliso School: "For the Mexican Children."* Santa Barbara: McSeas Books, 2003.

O'Connor, Alan. *Gold on the Diamond: Sacramento's Great Baseball Players, 1886–1976*. Sacramento: Big Tomato Press, 2008.

Ornelas, Michael R. *The Sons of Guadalupe: Voices of the Vietnam Generation and Their Journey Home*. San Francisco: Aplomb Publishing, 2009.

Ponce, Mary Helen. *Hoyt Street: An Autobiography*. Albuquerque: University of New Mexico Press, 1993.

Santillán, Richard A., et al. *Mexican American Baseball in the Inland Empire*. Charleston, SC: Arcadia Publishing, 2012.

———, et al. *Mexican American Baseball in Orange County*. Charleston, SC: Arcadia Publishing, 2013.

Zierer, Clifford Maynard. *San Fernando: A Type of Southern California Town*. Washington, DC: Association of American Geographers, 1934.